You need a new hip

George Williams

Table of Contents

Dancing Again

On a Saturday night in April 2015, my wife and I went to a social dance evening. This might not sound at all extraordinary, but this was the first time we had been dancing properly in nearly three years.

It's a long story, but three years earlier I had been to my doctor to ask for help to sort out a pain in my groin. It was a year later before a surgeon finally told me that I needed a new hip.

Being interested in knowing what was going to happen to me, I researched the internet and looked for blogs that might enlighten me. I found a lot of information and several blogs, but the technical information seemed targeted at medical students, and blogs rarely went beyond a few weeks after the surgery.

Whatever was going to happen to me, I decided to keep a diary of my experiences. I could then make them available to other people with a similar curiosity about what was happening to their bodies.

I published several blog entries but very few people seemed interested: perhaps blogs were the wrong medium for people about to have a hip replacement. The procedure is most common amongst older age groups, who are not necessarily, fans of the internet. So I decided to chronicle my experiences as a short book. This was in the hope that a few people with the same diagnosis can gain some idea of what is going to happen to them, as well as having an idea about how my recovery went.

Hip Replacement Facts

In the UK the National Health Service performs a massive number of hip replacements every year. For example, in 2013 there were 66,000 such operations. In other words, about 1,300 hips are being changed each week, or putting it another way, it means that one in every 1,000 people in Britain have a new hip each year...scary!

Considering that the typical person getting a new hip is most likely to be at least in their fifties or sixties, the numbers are indicating that quite a high proportion of people could end up with a lump of titanium in their thigh.

There are different types of replacement, partial or full, and the prosthesis inserted may be of a different construction to suit a particular need. They used to have a relatively short life, and could well have needed replacing again in five to ten years. Techniques and materials are improving all the time, and my surgeon suggested that mine could last for my lifetime, assuming I don't do anything silly. Now, surgeons don't carry out this operation unless it is really necessary, as even with hopefully a ten-year life it often means that some people have to have a second replacement as they grow older. The modern thinking is to try and avoid giving new hips until people are nearing the age of sixty, unless there is a serious issue.

Ignoring the emergency replacements from trauma situations, the symptoms of someone requiring a hip replacement vary, but it always involves pain. A lot of people I have spoken to seem to have suffered pain in the groin, or the thigh area, and also in the backside. There is also sometimes a feeling that the leg might collapse beneath you when walking or twisting. Movement can be restricted as the joint's flexibility suffers, and it is quite common for people to limp.

Because you may not suffer from all of the symptoms, there can be times, as with me, when a problem with the hip is never suspected. Even

You need a new hip

with arthritis that had been giving me painful joints for over 30 years, I never considered the possibility of needing a hip replaced. In fact having had several pain killing injections and arthroscopy on my knee 20 years ago, I always assumed that my knees would be the first joints to wear out and need replacing at some stage.

My messages here might sound alarming, but don't worry: if you wake up one morning with a stiff leg it doesn't mean you will definitely need a new hip. Please do not panic: if you have a good diet, keep your weight down, stay active but avoid sport that puts stress on joints, you can quite probably expect to have your own hips until mortality wins.

On the other hand if you are one of the unlucky ones and a surgeon has hinted at, or suggested that a new hip is needed, then this little book might prepare you for the next few months, and help to settle your nerves.▯

Three Years Ago

My story starts in 2012 when my wife, Deb, and I were on a cruise that went all around the world. It was a retirement present to ourselves and a sensational way to throw off the shackles of work, and we saw many marvellous things that have left an indelible impression in our minds. Anyway, the cruise is not the reason for this book but it was the moment that I first realised something was wrong.

I have always been a competitive person, and while on the ship I regularly played a version of cricket in the sports nets. I can't simply play a game without giving it my all, and I always jumped and ran around more than perhaps I should have done. After many years of joint issues, and having been diagnosed with osteoarthritis, I would have been better off restricting my activities to less energetic pastimes, but I enjoy taking part in sports. Although I was thoroughly enjoying the cricket, it was making me ache, and one evening when I got up from the dinner table I immediately collapsed back onto the chair as my leg gave way. To be honest this was an issue with my knee, but it was a warning sign.

Later in the cruise I made another serious error by joining in with a dance called 'Oops upside your head' that involves sitting on the floor with your legs stretched out to the side behind the person in front. After the dance was over most people stood up and returned to their drinks with ease, but I was stuck. I had to roll over onto my side and then stand up awkwardly before limping back to Deb for sympathy.

I didn't get any.

The next morning for the first time I noticed a tightening in my groin and an ache that was made worse by any form of movement. Now it's unlikely, and downright improbable, that the dance was the sole cause of the chain of events that were to follow, but that was the moment when my troubles first manifested themselves.

You need a new hip

Back home after the cruise I struggled for a few days before eventually going to see my GP. I thought I had strained a muscle in my thigh and he agreed with me, telling me to rest my leg and take painkillers. A couple of weeks later, and with no improvement, I returned to the doctor who now came to the conclusion that it might be a hernia.

This resulted in me being sent to have a scan in Stafford Hospital.

About a month later I had an ultra-sound scan and the operator advised me that I did have a small hernia in my groin area called an 'Inguinal Hernia'. The findings would be sent to the team dealing with this form of medical problem and they would arrange an appointment for me to see them.

I now started the National Health Service's 'six week' delay period. This appears to be a built-in waiting time between all investigations or treatments.

After the allotted waiting period I saw the consultant (or maybe it was his registrar) at Stafford hospital again. He listened to me for a while before proceeding to poke and probe my groin. Unconvinced, his next move was to grab my right leg and push and waggle it around making me wince with pain. My less-than-sympathetic surgeon sat me down and suggested that the hernia was not significant enough to be causing the pain, and he thought that there might be a problem with my hip. This was not what I expected, and in fact I was totally gobsmacked. The outcome of that 10-minute meeting was that an appointment would be made for me to see an orthopaedic consultant.

Six weeks later I was now visiting Cannock Hospital to see another consultant. It was definitely his registrar this time, a Mr Collier. His initial actions were to send me for x-rays of my hips and knees. On my return from the photo-shoot, Mr Collier looked at the x-rays and said that one knee was beyond treatment because of arthritic wear, but not so bad that it needed replacement. The right hip also had what he called *"an issue"*

You need a new hip

and although it was not badly affected it might be the reason for the pain I was suffering.

We talked for a moment and he said he was not sure if the pain was coming from the hip or from the hernia. The only way to find out was to give me a pain-killing injection into my hip and see if that made me more comfortable. If the pain didn't ease then the cause was probably the hernia, on the other hand if the pain reduced then it pointed to the hip issue, and I might eventually need a replacement.

I was truly shocked as I realised he was saying that I might require a new hip in the near future.

Up until that moment I thought I had a strained muscle, or perhaps had a hernia. Now I suddenly discovered that I might be heading for major surgery and a lump of metal being inserted in my leg.

It was the end of October 2012 and nearly six months since the first visit to see my GP.

Pain-Killing Injection

Fast forwarding about six weeks (again) to 4th December 2012, and I was booking myself into Cannock Hospital to have an injection in my right hip to try and confirm what was causing the pain in my groin area. This was no ordinary 'sharp scratch' injection and had to be given in a sterile environment with the aid of an x-ray machine to monitor the needle position.

Now these injections are a relatively quick and simple job, and in a typical orthopaedic surgical session they might perform two or three of them. But they are usually mixed in with various other exploratory procedures, plus possibly knee or hip replacements, so there was no way of predicting how long I would have to wait before actually having my injection. Hence once in the surgical area I sat impatiently dressed in my wonderful NHS operating gown that I can never tie up.

It was near the end of the afternoon when I had the call to wander down the corridor with a nurse and climb up on an operating table. There were a lot of people in the room all wearing gowns, and the major players also wore protective suits to avoid a dose of the x-ray radiation. Fortunately the screen with the picture of my hip was turned away from me so I didn't have to watch the seriously long needle going into the joint.

The first stage of the procedure was a quick dose of anaesthetic into the thigh and even that was rather painful. I was warned that I would feel the pressure of the main needle as it went in, and it proved to be a very strange sensation. I wasn't aware of doing it, but I had subconsciously decided to hold my breath. My attentive nurse gently took my hand and quietly suggested that I should breathe again now. The whole thing was over quite quickly, but the relief that it was done made me feel cold and I began to shiver. As I waited to be taken away on a trolley the wonderfully attentive nurses covered me with a blanket to try and warm me up.

You need a new hip

I suppose it was less than fifteen minutes from walking in until I was rolled out to recover with a cup of tea. In case of any strange reactions to the anaesthetic I had to have my blood pressure monitored, and I was kept still until they were sure I was OK.

Deb had to come and drive me home as my leg wouldn't be fully under my control for several hours. As the anaesthetic wore off later that evening I felt the pain caused by someone sticking something the size of a knitting needle through my thigh and into quite a large joint. It took several days for that initial pain to go away before I could start to decide if the injection had actually reduced the discomfort.

Finally there was one magic day when I made a discovery and exclaimed to Deb that I was not feeling any pain in the area of my groin. This was my first pain-free moment since this had all started around nine months before. Unfortunately my euphoria was not to last very long because the painkiller eventually started to wear off and little by little my troubles returned.

On January 14th 2013 (six weeks later again) I had a review appointment, and this time it was with the orthopaedic consultant, Mr Shaylor. I was able to tell him that the pain in my groin had definitely reduced after the injection, although it had now come back. To add to my woes, because I had been careful to avoid overusing the right leg, my left knee was now hurting very badly and in fact that pain was masking much of the issues with my hip.

The consultant decided to do two things. Firstly I was booked in to have an MRI scan of the hip to check if anything could be done to avoid a replacement. Secondly I would have an arthroscopy of my left knee to check for, and remove, any debris that might be floating around.

As I left the clinic I wondered how long it would be before I got these appointments.

Arthroscopy and MRI

Much to my surprise I was offered an appointment to have the arthroscopy of my left knee just a couple of weeks later on 1st February.

This was only minor surgery but I had to have all the routine health questions, plus blood pressure checks and swabs taken from various areas of my body to ensure I was clear of nasty bugs. Having cleared that hurdle I checked in at Cannock Hospital on Friday 1st February and was soon waiting in my backless gown for the call to the operating theatre again.

Before long I was following a nurse into the annex room of the operating theatre where the anaesthetist stuck a cannula in one arm, and a blood pressure cuff around the other. I had received a general anaesthetic before but I was quite worried as the liquid was pushed into my arm. I remember thinking that it was rather cold as it went in, but knew nothing else until I heard the sound of a nurse gently calling my name.

The poke around inside my left knee was completed and I was coming around in the recovery area. My knee was wrapped in a large dressing and I could hear the 'beeps' of the blood pressure monitor. I also noticed there was a drip in my arm receiving some fluid from a bag above me. Apparently my blood pressure had dropped quite low so they were giving me a top-up. After a few minutes I was making sense of what was going on around me, and when a cup of tea and a slice of toast was offered, I happily gobbled then down.

Well, I hadn't eaten anything since the previous night.

My blood pressure quickly returned to an acceptable reading and the nurses were happy that I was fully conscious and able to eat and drink. They removed the wadding around my knee and replaced it with a pair of simple adhesive dressings covering a tiny hole on either side of my knee. A phone call was made to ask Deb to come and collect me, and I was allowed to get dressed and sent to the waiting area with a letter to take to my GP, with instructions to watch out for any complications. An arthroscopy is a simple keyhole surgical procedure that just takes a few minutes and is done as a day case. So less than four hours after arriving at the hospital I was going home again.

My knee was sore and stiff and that first evening consisted of hobbling around and eating lots of food. I also had an early night to give my body time to clear itself of the anaesthetic.

After a couple of days I was recovering from my minor operation and was ready for the next adventure of an MRI scan that I was to have the following week.

Early on the morning of 8th February 2013 I was back at Cannock Hospital and waiting outside the MRI department ten minutes before my appointment. I discovered the staff had not arrived yet, so I hung around outside in the cold until the cheerful staff arrived and booked me in. First on the list, I was soon lying flat on the scanner bed and being trundled into the tube for 20 minutes of internal photography. Anyone who has had an MRI scan will know the experience I had, whilst for others who are luckily in ignorance of an MRI scan, let me try and describe it.

Imagine being in a horizontal tube that is quite narrow, and having to lie perfectly still for at least 20 minutes. Your view is limited and in reality you end up staring at the curved roof of the scanner which is no more than a few centimetres above your head. A pair of headphones is put over your ears: the first time I had this done music was played, but not this time. The machine starts to work and you quickly realise why the headphones have been supplied. There's a series of very loud noises as magnetic pulses blast at your body. These noises are loud and certainly not pleasant, so here are a few examples of what they sound like.

Firstly, imagine a heavy metal band where the guitarist is playing a loud and really unpleasant solo of a repetitive series of notes with no melody. This goes on without change for more than two minutes.

You need a new hip

Secondly, how about sticking your head into the engine compartment of a particularly noisy diesel lorry for a similar period of time?

Or maybe you would prefer the sound of a pig squealing continually, or someone trying to kick-start a motorbike.

These noises blast into your head for most of the time you are in the tube, and I can promise that it's a real relief when the headphones (completely useless at drowning out the sounds) eventually crackle into life to tell you that the scan is finished.

Fortunately my scan was soon over and I was on my way home within 45 minutes of arriving, and this time there was no residual pain from the morning's episode.

Three weeks later (27th February) I was sitting with Mr Collier (my surgeon) to discuss the outcomes of the arthroscopy on my knee and the MRI scan of my hip. My knee was moving towards a point where it would need to be replaced. But in the meantime he wanted to try one last thing to delay a replacement by injecting some artificial lubrication (called hyaluronan) into the knee joint. This substance had apparently shown good results and typically reduced pain for up to six months.

Turning to the question of my hip he said the MRI scan didn't show any unusual problems but neither did it suggest any further treatment was possible...

...except for a replacement.

Well, it was time to wait for the anticipated six weeks delay now before getting the next round of treatment.

I wonder if the NHS actually thinks we're not aware that there always seems to be the same duration between appointments for consultations and treatment.

A Self-Inflicted Delay

During March and April I was suffering worse and worse pain from my knee. It was masking the hip issues, and I was really very depressed by the constant ache even after taking maximum daily doses of pain-killing tablets. I had already moved from regular paracetamol to co-codamol, but any relief was minimal.

There was now an added problem to contend with.

We had made a decision several months earlier to move house. We'd found a property in Herefordshire, and we had buyers for our present house. We were planning and hoping for a moving date in April, which was when I suspected my next visit to see the surgeon would be, but I was quite prepared to come back to Staffordshire for the appointment if the move had already gone ahead.

Yes, this was going to impact on any further treatment, but I assumed (mistakenly) that the NHS was, as the name suggests, a National Health Service and I would be able to transfer my problems to the new health authority in Herefordshire, and continue from whatever point I had reached in Staffordshire. Of course I expected there would be some delay, and a few extra periods of six weeks to wait, but surely this would only be a small issue. In the meantime I did various physiotherapy exercises to strengthen the knee muscles, and counted down the days to my next visit to Cannock Hospital.

My appointment for the knee lubricant injection eventually arrived in the post, and was for 18th April. Problems with the people buying our house meant that we were still living in Staffordshire at that time. The injection would be given with just local anaesthetic, but would be carried out in the operating theatre again to maintain sterile conditions as the injection was going deep into my knee. At midday Deb dropped me off at the hospital and I was soon dressed in another ridiculous operating gown waiting for the nurse to come and collect me.

You need a new hip

When I was lying on the operating table, with one surgeon preparing me and then giving me the injection of artificial synovial fluid, several other surgeons including Mr Collier were chatting as they checked through their afternoon's operating list. Well, the injection wasn't too painful and as I waited for the porter to come and take me away, Mr Collier said he hoped that the injection would give me six months relief for the knee, and then discussed my move to Herefordshire. He prepared a letter, on behalf of the consultant, for me to hand to my new GP about the diagnosis and treatments given.

I thanked him for his efforts and asked what the situation was with my hip as nothing had been said about that for a while.

Quite flippantly he replied that there was no more simple treatment available and his final words to me were…

…*"You need a new hip"*.

That was my final experience with the North Staffordshire Health Trust. It had taken eleven months to finally arrive at this point of discovering that I needed quite a serious operation in the near future for what I originally thought was a simple strained muscle in my thigh.

Moving from Staffordshire to Herefordshire

After several weeks of delay Deb and I left the beautiful canal town of Stone in Staffordshire and moved to our new home in a lovely village about five miles from the city of Hereford. This was a new beginning for us, and any aches and pains were temporarily forgotten with the help of serious doses of co-codamol.

Within the first few days we both went to the surgery in the village and registered with a new doctor. At that first meeting with the doctor I described my troubles and what had been done so far. My new GP was quite apologetic but said little could be done until my notes were transferred from our old practice, and that might take a few weeks. I immediately thought *"six weeks again"*, but amazingly it was only four weeks before my doctor could finally look at what had happened.

He looked at the situation and immediately decided that my knee was probably the priority. It appeared that the NHS was now using a new delaying tactic before I could see a consultant. I had to fill out a self-assessment tick-sheet form to describe what my problem was, plus its severity and effect on my way of life.

This was the moment when I realised that the National Health Service is not as 'National' as I thought it should be. It seems that a diagnosis from a consultant in one Health Authority is not sufficient in another authority, and I was fundamentally starting all over again.

It was more than three months later, on 29th August 2013, that I sat in the waiting room of the orthopaedic outpatient clinic in Hereford Hospital to see my new consultant, Mr Oakley. He was a very nice man but extremely busy. Our first discussion proved a disaster as there were no notes or x-rays from Staffordshire.

I really was starting again.

You need a new hip

I had x-rays of hip and knee taken and then had another chat to Mr Oakley. His assessment was that he couldn't see any reason for me to have a new knee or a new hip at that moment. I explained to him what had been done and what I had been told, and although slightly less negative he remained sceptical. He said he would contact Staffordshire and ask for the notes to be sent to him. When he had them a new appointment would be made for me to see him.

Yes, you guessed it...this was going to take about six weeks.

My pain-killing co-codamol was now at the highest dose I was allowed to take, and I was in serious pain every day from both my knee and my hip. It was worse now than it had ever been, and I was in sickening pain all day.

A new start in Herefordshire

Even with the annoying delay to my treatment I was still confident that whatever was going to be done would be all done and dusted in a few months, so Deb and I now made a serious decision.

In September of 2013 we booked another world cruise that would leave Britain in January 2015 and give us a repeat of our adventure in 2012. We went to the Cruise Show at the NEC in Birmingham and sat with a cruise consultant who talked through the different options and eventually we walked away having paid a £1,500 deposit towards the £27,000 cost of our cabin. Yes, this was a lot of money to spend, but we had decided long ago that we would enjoy whatever life we had left as long as there was enough money remaining in the bank for our future needs.

So we now had a target for me to be repaired and ready for 15 months' time to sail around the world on the wonderful P&O ship *Arcadia*.

Surely that was plenty of time to get my hip sorted out?

It was a long wait for my next appointment with Mr Oakley. The mysterious six week delay had been and gone, and it was nearly 11 weeks later that I went back to Hereford Hospital on 7th November. Mr Oakley was now armed with my notes from Staffordshire and I knew he had a letter from the previous surgeon saying that I should be given a new hip when I decided the pain was too much. Unfortunately my new consultant was not convinced and wanted to be sure it was my hip causing the problem and suggested I have a pain-killing injection...

Aghh, I really was starting all over again!!

There was another wait now for the appointment for the injection.

Fortunately the wait was not very long and soon I was lying on the operating table having a large dose of pain-killer injected into my hip. I knew the routine and breathed throughout the procedure without the need for a nurse to remind me. This time I did have the x-ray screen turned in my direction and was invited to look at the offending hip with a needle stuck in it. Yes, I did look, and was not overly impressed with the photographer, but it did show clearly how long the needle had to be to get right into the joint.

To shorten this story just a little, the injection worked and almost immediately I had relief for a couple of weeks. I was quite sure that I was heading for a new hip, and waited for the letter to arrive with my next appointment.

Mr Oakley had suggested my review meeting would be soon after the injection, but the first date I was given was several weeks later, for the 6th March 2014. Worse still, this was then cancelled and replaced by another on the 20th March. I was now in severe pain again, and rang the hospital to point out that I had been promised an appointment much earlier than the date I was given. Just as I was thinking that there was never any good news, Mr Oakley's secretary looked at the diary and asked if I could accept an appointment that had come available for 27th February. Bloody stupid question, I accepted it immediately before anyone changed their minds.

So just before the end of February 2014 I was sitting in a small office with one of Mr Oakley's registrars. He asked me if the injection had made any difference and I told him that the pain was reduced significantly for about two or three weeks, but that it was back now. This was obviously the correct response, as he pointed out that the injection contained a short duration drug. We chatted through how I felt and then he spent a minute or two looking through my notes.

The folder he was reading was closed and he said that if I was ready for it I could go on the waiting list for a total hip replacement.

You need a new hip

He asked me if I had any questions, but apart from asking what I would be able to do or not do afterwards, I was really over the moon that an end to the pain was at last on the horizon. He read through a form about the possible risks and side effects of the operation, and then sought my agreement by signing the initial consent form. When I asked about the waiting time he was not very forthcoming, but the suggestion was of at least two months before my name would be getting to the top of the list.

It may appear to be a surprising reaction but I was just so very happy as I left the hospital that day, even though I knew I was about to have a major operation in the near future.

I had finally got further on in the process than I had in Staffordshire, but it had taken another ten months from when Mr Collier had said the same thing.

A Busy Period

I knew that the impending operation would affect my mobility and restrict me to light duties. So I set about completing all the outstanding jobs around the house, as well as making sure the garden was ready for our vegetables. There were several little DIY jobs that hadn't been completed that now became urgent. One was a serious need to construct a shower, as I knew I wouldn't be able to have a bath for several weeks after my appointment with the surgeon. We already had a shower over the bath but getting in and out of the bath would be an impossible manoeuvre, so a stand-alone shower cubicle was required.

This was temporarily constructed in the corner of the garage where I had already provided plumbing for the washing machine. I spent several weeks looking for a suitable shower cubicle and chose one that we hoped could eventually be made a permanent feature in an area of the house we had planned as a shower room. The construction was quite simple and before I received a date for the operation it was in and ready for use.

Six weeks had already passed and I had not received an appointment yet.

I did have to attend a clinic in the hospital for people about to have a joint replacement, so I knew things were happening. This clinic had two purposes. The first part assessed my fitness for surgery, with swabs being taken from various bits of my body in order to check that I wasn't carrying any nasty little bugs. The next part of the clinic was a talk by a nurse about the operation, and I was even shown an example of the titanium prosthesis that would be inserted into my leg, plus the ceramic cup that would replace the existing hip socket. This was quite fascinating but just a little bit scary.

For several weeks after the operation there was going to be a number of things that I would be unable to do, or strictly banned from attempting.

If I didn't stick to these rules there was a possibility of dislocating the new hip, or even damaging it.

- Firstly I would be walking with crutches for at least six weeks while the muscles in my thigh recovered, and the bone in my leg started to regenerate to cover the prosthesis.

- Crossing my legs was banned, and bending was to be very limited.

- I had to be careful never to allow my hip to be lower than my knee when I sat.

- Finally, and the most serious of all the restrictions, was that I had to sleep on my back for six weeks, and not to attempt rolling onto my side, or allowing my leg to turn outwards while I slept.

To get me ready the nurses asked me about our toilets, and heights of furniture above the ground. I would be supplied with a toilet seat riser and also a frame, or perching stool, to enable me to wash whilst sitting at a sink. But it was my responsibility to ensure any chairs I would be using were high enough, and also that the height of our bed was suitable to avoid any over-bending of my knee.

As a result of this discussion, we bought a second-hand chair from a charity shop and raised the seat area sufficiently with a block of foam. This became my personal comfortable chair for many weeks. We also replaced the mattress on our bed for one that was significantly thicker than the old one, and hence the bed was now high enough. This was something we had planned to buy anyway.

What with the shower, the mattress and a new chair, this operation was proving to be quite an expensive hit to our savings.

Then one morning the letter arrived, and I finally had a date for my operation. It was to be Tuesday 17th June 2014.

You need a new hip

With all our jobs around the house and garden completed we made the most of the remaining weeks to go and visit my family in Cornwall, and then we booked a short cruise to spoil ourselves for a week.

Talking of cruises, I was just a little concerned that there wouldn't be long enough after the operation to get myself sufficiently mobile before our planned world cruise in January 2015. After asking various people and looking on the internet it seems I would be fine after six months.

Panic over!!

During May I had to go back to the hospital clinic to check I was fit enough and free from bugs again because it had been so long since the previous checks. This was the fourth time that I had been through this health check in two years.

Days and weeks ticked by and we enjoyed a beautiful early summer sitting in the garden or exploring the city of Hereford and the surrounding countryside. At the beginning of May we had our cruise down to Spain knowing that the next time we boarded a ship would be starting our adventure around the world.

Perhaps this is the moment to describe just how I was feeling with just four weeks to go before my hip would be replaced.

To put it simply I was in pain every day.

The original pain in my groin area was almost constant, but there were other areas of my leg that made life so difficult. There was an ache in my backside as if I had been sitting on something hard for a long time. I spent a lot of time with an ache deep inside my leg that I couldn't pinpoint, but it was somewhere between my hip and my knee. It was the sort of ache that you want to rub to make it feel better, but I just couldn't find the spot to rub. Although I could walk it was hardly more than 100 metres before the ache in my leg increased, and it became worse if I twisted the leg or misjudged stepping on or off the kerb. Sometimes I felt a strange sensation that my leg might give way if I put too much weight on it.

You need a new hip

Putting all these symptoms together I realised I was limping as I favoured the right leg. Of course that made the pain in my left knee worse.

You have to realise that on a scale of 1 to 10 my overall pain was perhaps around 6 to 7, so not the worst I had ever felt. But the major issue was that it was there for most of my waking day, and didn't improve much when I went to bed. I was taking pain-killers like they were sweets, and I often clock-watched to see when I could have some more. I tried pain relieving gels without much success, and went through phases of hot water bottles or ice-packs in attempts to find something that might give me a few hours relief. I regularly groaned as I stood up or sat down and Deb was used to me wincing if I moved too quickly.

A lot of people asked how I was getting on and showed concern that I was about to have quite a big operation. My reply was quite short and simple...

..."*I had had enough pain and was ready for the operation*".

Tuesday 17th June 2014

It was over two years since I first went to see my GP in Staffordshire to complain about an ache in my groin. Moving house obviously delayed treatment, but I don't think that Aneurin Bevan's vision of a National Health Service involved such a lack of trust between a consultant in one health authority to another less than 100 miles away. I also think Bevan might have laughed at the seemingly compulsory six week (or more) delay between consultations or treatments. I know the service is swamped by demand, and there must be waiting lists and priorities, but successive governments have increased budgets in attempts to speed up the system and yet this mysterious period of six weeks doesn't seem to be changing.

Anyway, at last it was my turn, and after having had no food since the previous evening and only a sip of water to take my morning pills, I arrived at Hereford Hospital just after midday. As Deb and I sat in the waiting room of the surgical ward we saw several other people sheepishly arriving and being told to take a seat. Some would be having injections or arthroscopies, but some would be waiting for something a little more serious and having a new knee or a new hip like myself.

The waiting room began to fill and eventually I was called by a nurse to go into a little side room to start the ball rolling. I had my blood pressure checked and I put on the back-to-front gown which, for a change, was tied up properly by Deb. Next, I had a compression sock put on the leg not being operated on. This was all part of the prevention to stop me getting Deep Vein Thrombosis issues, and after the operation I would have one put on the other leg as well. Things were getting serious now, so Deb gave me a kiss and wished me the best before leaving me to panic and worry on my own about what was going to happen.

One of the surgical team came and drew a big arrow pointing to my right hip and wrote the word 'hip' on the thigh. I also signed a confirmation of my consent for the operation.

You need a new hip

It was just after 1:00 pm and things went very quiet for a while. Nurses occasionally popped in to see if I was alright and I asked when something might happen. They checked the running order but couldn't give me any indication of how long I would be waiting. At 2:00 pm my anaesthetist came into the room and quickly went through a few of the things that he would be doing. It didn't mean anything to me, but the important bit was that as he left he said it would be about another 30 minutes.

Sure enough, at 2:30 pm a nurse collected me and took me to the preparation annex room of the operating theatre. As the nurse chatted to me to keep me calm I noticed my anaesthetist was preparing a kidney dish full of various drugs, chemicals and potions to inject into my body. He took centre stage now, and after the warning of a *"sharp scratch"* he inserted a cannula into one arm while his assistant wrapped a blood pressure cuff around the other. The cocktail of drugs I was about to have included antibiotics and something to reduce my blood pressure during the operation. I was also going to have a spinal block and was expecting to have to sit while that was given to me. Anyway, I had a couple of shots of liquid pushed into my veins and then I was asked to roll onto my side. When I was steady there was another surge of cold liquid going up my arm...

.....and that was the last thing I remembered.

My next recollection was about two hours later at 5:00 pm with a recovery nurse talking to me gently to bring me out of my temporary coma. I was completely disorientated, sore, and unsure of what had happened. I was lying on my back with a hissing sound of oxygen-enriched air being blown into my nose, and although I was aware that something was different around my thigh area, it was giving me no pain. A drip in my left arm was bringing my fluid level up. The modern thinking is to reduce the body's blood pressure before an operation, as well as thinning the blood. Hence the first priority was to get that pressure back up to normal levels again.

You need a new hip

As soon as I was speaking reasonably rationally I was wheeled to my new home in Teme Ward, where I joined another patient, Clive, who I eventually learned had received a new hip a few days earlier. He was significantly older than me and struggling with his recovery especially after falling over. There were two empty beds in our little room that would stay empty until the following day.

Nurses came and went, and the blood pressure monitor was continually checking my progress. I took my first sips of water, but without any real enthusiasm, as my only desire was to sleep off the experience I had just gone through that had exhausted me.

All seemed to be going to plan until a young Italian nurse asked if I had any pain. I replied that I was hurting at the lower end of my stomach. Realising I was so full of pain-killer that I shouldn't have been able to feel anything, he became concerned.

He asked if I had any desire to pass water. Not understanding the connection I said no. He carefully pressed on my stomach, and the wince and yelp of pain that I gave was obviously not good. After five minutes I had a bladder scan and within another thirty minutes I had a catheter fitted to reduce the 1.5 litres of urine that I had accumulated in my bladder. That little adventure wasn't pleasant, and my dignity had been further destroyed, with seemingly no part of my body under my control any more.

But relief was quite quick, and soon I was able to allow the nurse to press on my stomach without discomfort.

I was not expecting Deb to visit me that evening but I had a message that she had called to ask how I was. The evening passed with regular blood pressure checks, a further bottle of fluid hooked up to my arm and a late-night snack of pain-killers to top me up.

Sleep was not going to be easy as I was now becoming aware of the thigh and feeling very uncomfortable. I had to sleep on my back and my right leg was protected in a trough to avoid any chance of me trying to move it. They needn't have been concerned as I had no control over it with my muscles completely useless.

As the evening shift swapped to the night I met some new faces, and one asked if I was hungry. Having not eaten for 15 hours that was a stupid question, and she organised a sandwich for me. As I received it she also gave me a sick bowl with the words that I would probably need that as well. Well fortunately she was wrong, and although I didn't eat more than half of the tasty ham sandwich, it stayed inside my stomach and I felt just a little better.

Of course it was now one of the hottest periods of the year and it was so difficult to get any sleep, but there were brief moments of relief. Sadly, I also discovered that Clive was not only older but he struggled with his mind as well, and took part in several random discussions with himself during the night. But at least he didn't snore.

During the many waking moments through the night my head was full of questions and concerns about what the next few days would bring.

Recovery Begins

I was rather pleased when the ward came to life the next morning. It was early, but already the sun had been streaming through the window for a couple of hours. Sleep had been illusive but I did manage a few naps as I turned my head from side to side to find a cool bit of the pillow. My leg had stayed still all night with my foot pointing up, but even if I had any inclination to try and move it I would have failed, as I had no muscular control over my right leg at all.

One of the last jobs of the night shift sister was to give me my regular prescription pills, together with some pain relief. I was asked if I had a preference for what type of morphine I wanted. Having never had it before (to my knowledge) I just stared back at her blankly, and she made the choice for me.

After pills and sips of water I dozed off again, but not for long as just after 6:00 am the horrendous rattle of the observation trolley heralded my first check of the day. I did have fleeting memories of having checks during the night, but I had been too drowsy to pay attention or worry about them.

The next thrill was breakfast at 7:00 am. I just had a bowl of bran flakes and a cup of tea. It may have been a simple meal but my stomach was extremely happy to receive it.

As the day shift took over the ward I had my urine bag emptied and taken away for measurement of my output (yes crude isn't it?). It seems that so far I had produced over two and a half litres, which was making my tummy feel much, much better. It's a strange feeling passing water with no effort, and in fact, no awareness for most of the time. I was more concerned about when the catheter had to be removed.

Next it was time for a wash and I was sat up in bed with my wash kit and a bowl of warm water, plus instructions to do as much as I could. It

You need a new hip

was good to realise that I could do something for myself on the first day. Pleased with my efforts, the nurses came back and completed my wash with a bed bath.

More of my dignity gone

After that, an elastic surgical stocking was applied to my right leg to join the one that was put on my left leg before surgery. This was all about reducing the risk of deep vein thrombosis, which can occur when lying around in hospital. The previous night I also had an injection in my stomach to thin the blood as a post-surgical procedure, and that would continue for some time as the risk of thrombosis is quite high.

Other highlights included a fleeting visit from a doctor who was a part of the surgical team. It was just a courtesy visit as he did nothing apart from ask me how I was. After that a lady came and took some blood from me. I've never been happy about needles or having blood taken, but this was much less painful than most things I had been through in the previous 24 hours.

Now came a less comfortable moment as a porter came to take me for an x-ray to check that the operation had been successful. He had a trolley with him that I realised I was going to be moved on to. A few nurses turned up to help as I was initially rolled onto my bad leg while a slider sheet was put under me. That was followed by the actual slide to the trolley. Both of these actions were extremely painful and I yelped quite loudly.

I think the nurses and porters are quite used to this.

The visit to the x-ray department was a nice change from the ward and caused me no grief. Of course on my return to the ward the move back to my bed was no less painful than getting off, but my yelps were slightly less dramatic.

Later I had the results of the x-ray and the new joint looks to be perfect.

You need a new hip

The morning ended with the physiotherapy team coaxing me out of my bed and onto my feet. Like a lot of people in this situation I had serious concerns that standing was going to be painful, and the titanium rod would break under my weight. Silly boy, the pain was minimal and the prosthesis was perfectly happy supporting my body. A little shaky and sore, I was turned and allowed to sit in my chair before the serious business when I tried to walk a few steps with the aid of a frame. It went as well as expected, and I took a few steps across the room before deciding the world was spinning and it was time to lie down again.

More observations

Lunch came at 12:30 pm and to be honest it was appalling. I had chosen a simple cottage pie and veg dish that turned out to be tasteless, with the pie being stodgy and the veg simply a pretty coloured alternative. I remember school meals being basic and unimpressive, but at least they tasted of something. What has happened to modern mass-catering kitchens??

At least the ice-cream was a good choice for a dessert.

After lunch the ward quietened down as visiting time neared, and I was looking forward to Deb coming in to see me. She spent almost an hour looking concerned as I lay painfully in front of her. We talked about the operation (or what I could remember) and my attempts at walking, and the lack of taste in the food. Deb was a bit shocked seeing a bag of urine beside my bed, but problems with passing water is a common issue after surgery with such strong anaesthetics in use. There was also a treat as Deb brought me some strawberries from our garden, as well as orange squash and a piece of home-made cake to supplement my diet.

While Deb was there, a new patient arrived opposite my bed. This was Chris who had just had a knee replacement and looked in the same sorry state as I had felt the previous evening. The only difference was the lump of bandage on his knee, and a drain from his leg collecting blood. This blood was later returned to his body through a drip. His surgeon believes this helps the recovery process, but it looked very strange and slightly weird.

With Deb gone I returned to the comfort of my pillow and dozed again. Not for long though, as the final patient for our section of the ward arrived soon after. This was Frank and he was another hip replacement. Nurses were going frantic now taking reading of blood pressure, oxygen levels, temperatures and pulse rates around our four beds. Meanwhile, with all the chaos going on around us, the older guy, Clive, sat quietly in a world of his own, apart from the occasional mumble of conversation with himself, and endless snippets of tunes that were coming into his head. This was Clive, and he did very little else.

There was another round of painkillers to keep me comfortable and soon it was 6:30 pm and supper time. My choice of sandwich was suitable, and a further pot of ice-cream was enhanced by the delicious (and tasty) fresh strawberries from home.

The evening was boring, except for Clive who was visited by his wife and daughter, and Chris who was joined by his partner for half an hour. I was tired and made the most of the time listening to some music and succumbing to a doze or two.

Handover between the staff meant it was now night-time and once the visitors had gone we had our observation trolley rattling around again, and a final visit by the painkiller fairy with paracetamol, plus a stronger pill and a sharp scratch into the stomach. Lights were dimmed and it was time to sleep again with my leg protected by my frame.

Now I discovered that as well as Clive singing and mumbling, Chris was an Olympic champion at snoring, with Frank a close second.

This was to be a long night with very little sleep.

Day 2

After an awful night with just a few minutes sleep I had stupidly become quite angry with the loud snorers. One in particular had an almost continuous sequence of a loud intake of breath (more of a gasp) followed by an explosive exhalation accompanied by a horrible wheeze. This went on for hours...and I do not exaggerate!

The other snorer only performed after being asleep for quite a while, and it was a simple (but loud) typical grating intake of breath.

Along with it being one of the hottest nights that we had that summer, I found it virtually impossible to get any extended restful sleep. I wished I was with the nurses in the corridor where they chatted between periods of activity attending to observations, answering requests for bedpans, replacing sheets, or just giving a bit of TLC to patients in pain or discomfort. The night shift appeared to be just three nurses to cover a ward with certainly more than15 beds of men and women at different stage of recovery after serious surgery.

The morning eventually took over proceedings with observations, painkillers and a chat to the ward sister completing her shift. Breakfast finally came to give stomachs relief, and by then the day shift had arrived with their duties sorted out according to each patients' needs.

It seemed that yesterday's blood test had shown my body clear of all the nasty chemicals that were causing my waterworks problems, so my catheter was removed and I was on my own again with that particular bodily function. My newly found skills at walking with a frame were then tested by the nurses as I was convinced to move to my chair where I had a bowl of water to wash myself. This was another step along the way to release from hospital that I had decided was my priority after the noisy night preventing me getting any rest.

You need a new hip

The surgical team arrived and let me know that my new joint is perfectly positioned and everything went fine during the operation.

Soon the physiotherapists returned to get me active again, and this time after a short stroll with the frame I was given my crutches and instructed to take my first steps. All went well initially but half way across the short ward I felt just a little dizzy.

That was enough for now.

The team took me back to the chair and I had some precautionary observations that must have shown I had done too much as I was left alone for the rest of the morning. The physiotherapy exercises did continue during the afternoon, and this time I felt far happier. My mobility with the crutches was far better than with the frame. I could now make my way to the toilet on my own, and wash at the sink instead of using a bowl. This was another major step along the path to recovery.

Amusement for the day was Frank's visit to the x-ray department. I knew the transfer to the trolley was a painful experience for him, but unlike my almost muted yelps, he screamed with an expletive about a digestive bi-product to demonstrate his unhappiness with the nurses' lack of compassion. I looked across at Chris and we were both giggling with tears in our eyes at Frank's performance. We also knew there would be a repeat performance when he came back...and there was!

Already angry with the world, Frank was visited by the physiotherapy team for his first outing with his frame. This was a disaster...except for me and Chris. He managed to get upright after several shrieks of pain, and was then coaxed into trying his first steps. Within five minutes he was flat on his bed, with oxygen to bring his blood pressure back up again. His recovery was going to be a long haul.

Visitors came and went, and disgusting meals filled a few minutes at lunchtime and early evening. The day turned to night and I lay again listening to the snores, plus occasional mumblings from Clive and the background babble of nurses and rumbles of trolleys.

You need a new hip

Yes I really did want to get well enough as soon as possible to go home.

Day 3 (Friday)

I was even more determined to get home as quickly as possible following another noisy, hot, and sleepless night.

Yesterday Deb had brought in my reaching stick (similar to those things to pick up litter) and shoehorn so I could now practice new skills. The occupational nurse showed me how to use my new toys, and also gave me a length of bandage so that I could use it to lasso my foot and then move my leg around. After a bit of coaxing and practice I was able to get myself out of bed. then pick up and put on my socks by using the reaching stick, plus a bit of foot manoeuvring with the bandage. The shoehorn also helped me to put on my slippers. The nurses had put my wash kit and my clothes for the day in a neat pile near enough to the bed for me to get at. So I was able to get up, dress, and walk to the bathroom on my crutches for a wash. I had a real sense of achievement and looked and felt more presentable...probably smelt better too.

Returning from the bathroom I sat myself down in the chair and waited for the daily arrivals into the ward. Sure enough, the blood sample lady came to collect a few millilitres from Clive and then the physiotherapists arrived. They concentrated on Chris initially getting him to lift his knee using the familiar length of bandage trick, as well as various exercises to strengthen his muscles. I had a further trot around the ward with my crutches and it was obvious that Chris and I were making progress while the other two were not.

Clive had now been in the ward for nine days, and today was the first time he was allowed back on crutches since an earlier aborted attempt when he fell over. He actually looked to be doing fine but carrying his urine bag around was a major obstacle to this style of movement.

Then it was Frank's turn. There were a few minutes of obscenities as he was forced to become vertical, and positioned between the arms of his frame. When asked to shuffle there was very little progress with his operated leg proving too heavy for his weakened muscles. He got as far as the end of his bed before a rapid return to bed and another intervention by nurses with the observation trolley and an oxygen mask.

My occupational therapist came and chatted through the things required at home in preparation for my discharge. I have what is known as a perching stool to allow me to sit at the sink and wash, as well as a toilet seat extension to avoid me having to sit too low and put stress on the hip. Unfortunately they had not been delivered yet so that was a minor delay to my going home.

A member of my consultant's team came and announced that everything has gone very well and I could go home as soon as everybody else agreed.

I still had to prove my ability to use crutches to go up and down stairs, and of course get confirmation of my bits and bobs being delivered to home. That didn't happen during Friday, so I knew that tomorrow was my new target date for discharge.

By now I was choosing the simplest meals from the menu, but the canteen even managed to make a cheese omelette look unappealing and taste of absolutely nothing. Fortunately I still had some strawberries from home to mix with the passable ice-cream.

Now there was one major mistake that I made during these couple of days. Each day someone would ask if we had passed water, to which I replied positively. The other question was about bowel movement, and here I was not performing. I couldn't lie, and admitted that nothing was happening, but when offered something to ease my problem I held on to the control of the last small area of my body and said "no thanks". With hindsight I wish I'd been sensible here, as the constipation was already bad and became a serious issue when I got home. It's a sad thing that we men try to avoid asking for, or accepting, the obvious help that is being offered.

You need a new hip

Friday quietly dragged through to the evening, and a further hot and noisy night beckoned. At least I had the very positive thought that tomorrow I would be going home.

Time to go home

I woke on Saturday morning after another painfully long, noisy, and hot night. Unless something seriously went wrong I would be going home today to sleep in my own bed without the noise of strangers and hospital sounds. There will just be my wonderful Deb beside me, and I have grown used to her sounds over the last 39 years, and any disturbance here would be minimal.

Anyway the day started as usual with painkillers at 6:00 am followed by breakfast an hour later. I was then sent packing towards the bathroom where one of the day shift nurses had taken my chosen clothes and wash kit. With no problems at all I picked up my crutches and made my way to the sink to shave and clean myself up to face the day. Unfortunately I dropped my dirty clothes and could not reach them so made my way back to my chair to wait for a nurse to bring back my debris.

Suddenly all hell broke loose!

An alarm went off in the distance and nurses stopped what they were doing and ran down the corridor. Someone had had a nasty turn and we heard later that his pulse rate had sunk to just 34 beats per minute. Within a couple of minutes various 'crash team' doctors and support staff ran into the ward and toward the incident. After a further couple of minutes some of the ward's nurses had been stood down from the emergency and were making their way back to us.

(The gentleman concerned was already suffering from a chest infection but recovered quite quickly from this major panic.)

My dirty washing was returned to me, and the rest of the walking wounded had their washes and got dressed for the day.

My bed was made and looked as though it shouldn't be disturbed, so the rest of my time on the ward was spent sitting in the chair or wandering around the room. I was given confirmation that I was

You need a new hip

scheduled to go today, so I rang Deb with the news but had no idea of exactly when I could leave. Opposite me, Chris was also extremely happy as he was planning to go home as well.

With observations completed, the physiotherapist arrived and started on Chris. He had to demonstrate certain levels of mobility, including going up and down steps, and after the initial checks in the ward he disappeared on a wheelchair towards the test staircase. Meanwhile the nurses were offering us a chance to soak our feet in a bowl of water, but I didn't take up this opportunity as I was expecting my turn with the stair test very soon. Actually, I could have enjoyed this treat, as it was quite a while before the physio man returned. Frank, in the bed next to me, sat quietly for several minutes paddling his feet before they were gently dried by the attentive young nurse.

My turn finally came to test my skills and I was whisked away to the staircase where I showed sufficient confidence and mobility to be trusted to climb up and down stairs. Back in the ward, I now had to wait for the duty doctor to sign me off as fit to go.

This took a long time to happen.

Morning coffee passed, and lunch was imminent, but I still had no idea if and when I would be going home.

The senior nurse checked and changed my dressing, as well as ensuring my records were up to date. She then turned her attention to Frank's dressing and this became the second major excitement for the morning. While standing to have the dressing replaced he fainted.

Alarms sounded and nurses ran from all directions and crowded into his curtained-off bed area. After a couple of minutes the curtains were drawn back to reveal Frank flat on his bed with a blood pressure monitor attached and oxygen mask over his face. This was becoming a daily occurrence for poor Frank.

You need a new hip

Lunchtime came and I chewed my way through my tasteless choice for the day and I didn't even have any strawberries left to have with my ice-cream. The ward goes quiet during the meals although today there was a slight background disturbance from Frank's oxygen supply.

Just before 2:00 pm I was told I could go home, and I rang Deb to ask her to come and collect me. To his disappointment Chris had to stay a little longer. His blood test showed a deficiency in potassium and this had to be rectified before he could be allowed home.

Stocked up with my bag of medicines, letters for GP and nurse, crutches and clothes, Deb wheeled me out as I said goodbye to my ward-mates and thanked the nurses as I passed by.

Getting into the car was a bit of a nightmare as it was really too low for the safe hip precautions that I had been instructed in, but I was soon perched on a cushion with my head nearly touching the car's roof as Deb drove me home.

Sunday and Monday at Home

My first night at home was far more pleasant than the experiences of lying awake in the hospital for hours on end. I did have to get up several times to go to the toilet, but it was so much more satisfying to be able to get up when I wanted to, rather than waiting for nurses to come along. After my first trip along the corridor in the dark to my plastic throne, Deb turned a light on to avoid me tripping on something, but in fact my crutch-work was improving and my confidence increasing.

Deb brought me breakfast in bed and after a little more snoozing I got up and sat at the sink on my perching stool to wash myself. More pleasure, as I know I could take my time without queues of others waiting for their turn.

I needed some help to dress but only to get things near enough for me to use my reaching tool to put them on. My leg was still very stiff and hurt if I moved it incorrectly or erratically, so the process of dressing was slow, but that rapidly improved as I had more practice at it. Unfortunately however, I still had to wear the horrible surgical compression stockings. These olive green stockings went from toes to knee and were uncomfortable, unsightly, and kept my legs far too hot. I really looked forward to them coming off permanently after a few weeks. The recommendation is that they should be worn for at least four weeks to reduce DVT issues.

Each morning after my wash I went downstairs and spent a few minutes on my laptop. On the Sunday Deb took the opportunity of me being comfortable to go to the supermarket for some bits and bobs. This included that laxative I mentioned, plus a treat of some grapes. We hadn't bought any for several years, and I quickly tucked into them.

The food cheered me up so much. It is amazing how a tasty meal can make you feel better. What a pity that hospitals don't seem to realise the recovery benefits of decent food.

The leg improved as I took regular walks into the garden and the stiffness eased. Unfortunately the bruise on my thigh was coming out and the staples holding my wound together were becoming very uncomfortable to sit on. My knee also became swollen from a lack of use while walking with crutches. It needed some frozen peas to regularly cool and reduce its size.

Climbing stairs became almost automatic, but I was careful not to get carried away. Coming down was worse, as the consequences of getting it wrong were visibly staring at me as I took my tentative steps.

After lunch I was getting into a routine of having an hour on my bed. This re-energised my body and gave the leg a chance to disperse the swelling a little. Sleep came easily both in the day and at night, but the constipation required far too many trips to the toilet, and getting comfortable again was not as easy as simply slumping back into the bed. I needed a support pillow under the knee, but that quickly became hot and required turning or swapping for a fresh pillow after each trot to the toilet. Similarly the pillows under my head became hot and needed regular turning.

On Monday morning I had a special treat when Deb washed my hair. I perched on my stool with my head leaning back into the shower (built in the garage). It was an unusual experience, and water went absolutely everywhere meaning a complete change of clothes was necessary. But it was oh so nice to have clean hair again.

On Monday afternoon there were two major landmark moments.

Firstly, just after lunch, the grapes, chocolate, and laxative finally worked and my personal waste disposal system was clear of the bad memories from the last few days. I still had a sore backside, but I was at last looking forward to slightly less traumatic visits to the toilet.

Secondly I got into the car again for a trip to the local surgery where the nurse inspected the operation wound for any sign of infection, and to check that it was beginning to heal. It was doing well with no indications of any problems, and was almost dry. She was gentle and the experience was painless, and I left a few minutes later with a fresh dressing. I would be back in a week for the staples to come out, and that would be the next major landmark with just a little while longer to wait before my first shower would be possible.

During Monday night the discomfort from my leg became unbearable and I had to get up and go downstairs for a while. The leg throbbed and I needed to move it every few minutes. There was not much scope for movement in bed and I was struggling to stay comfortable long enough to fall asleep. The continual fidgeting was also disturbing Deb far too much, and she deserved to rest after looking after me so wonderfully.

Downstairs I switched on my Kindle for the first time since going into hospital, and being happy to read again was another landmark. Whilst reading I realised my inability to do things. I could see some mixed nuts and raisins in a jar below the television and my taste buds were tingling. The problem was I couldn't reach down far enough to pick them up. That got sorted out the next day and they appeared on the side table by my chair with all my other necessities and treats.

After thirty minutes of reading I returned to bed and was fast asleep almost straight away. These middle of the night walks would become a common theme.

The second week

Tuesday 24th June
Just a week today since my operation

My morning started with Deb washing my hair again. I didn't get quite as wet all over as the first time, so our method was improving. I really enjoyed the experience because it made me feel so much fresher.

The weather was glorious, with hours of warm sunshine, so I took the opportunity to enjoy time in the garden. My chair was moved out onto the lawn so that I could look around like an ageing monarch surveying his kingdom. While I lazed, Deb dug up a row of potatoes and they were eventually stored in a hessian bag in the garage. This was the beginning of our main potato harvest, and all I could do was to watch and smile. Deb also half-filled a washing-up bowl with freshly-picked strawberries: we had enough that we were enjoying them with every meal. It couldn't have been a better choice after my days with hospital food.

I regularly grabbed my crutches and did a circuit or two of the garden. The plot is quite large and provided a challenging bit of exercise for the leg, making me just a little puffed with the effort. The leg felt stronger and my balance on the crutches improved to the point where I could get up quite a speed...but still with great care.

We had a visit from our immediate neighbours to say hello and ask how I was. They have been so good to us since we moved in a year ago and I couldn't be happier having them as neighbours.

As the bruising around my thigh was beginning to subside it brought me a further slight problem. The staples were now more prominent and when sitting down they occasionally gave me sharp pains, but I could avoid the worst of it by leaning to my left whenever I sat down. On the subject of sitting down, things were certainly improving as I now had the choice of two chairs to sit on. As well as my personal lounge chair I could

43

also sit at the dining table with a suitably cushion-softened chair allowing me to eat at the table...another small victory.

After lunch I continued to have a nap and this quiet moment gave me an opportunity to put a bag of frozen peas on my knee. It was noticeably swollen and reacting badly to the different actions that my leg had to make.

My nap breaks also started with the physio exercises. They were quite simple starting by paddling my feet back and forth followed by a series of pushing the back of my knee into the bed to bring the muscle groups into action. The third one was to clench and relax my buttocks and the final one was to attempt to lift my leg. When I first attempted this in hospital my brain asked the question but my leg remained still on the bed. As the days went by I was managing a lift of just an inch or two. This all helped with the actions needed to get in and out of bed. I was still using that length of bandage as a crane, but I hoped to get rid of it soon as my leg control improved.

Sleeping remained a problem with numerous trips to the toilet during the night. My painkiller regime focussed on the daytime, so when I got back into bed during the night I was in pain with no dose left to take. Deb continued to be so good with me and never hesitated to help me getting back into bed and rearranging my pillows.

What must it be like for single people in this situation??

Wednesday 25th June

I had a visit today from another neighbour in the road. She brought me a plastic 'Thomas the Tank Engine' football as a joke to encourage me to kick it around when I was better. I'm sure it'll be appreciated by our baby grandson when he gets a little older. The other immediate neighbours had chatted to me out in the garden while I continued to watch Deb dig and bag potatoes, as well as picking yet more strawberries.

My personal best today was to start laying the table when we eat. I had to move chairs and get mats, salt, pepper, and cutlery from the cupboard onto the table.

These are small achievements maybe, but all very positive.

Other exercises that I am expected to do include standing up and swinging my leg gently sideways from my body, and then backward and forwards a little bit. The target was to do these and the lying-down ones every hour, but I found that the leg ached quite seriously after each session and I couldn't keep up that schedule.

I was also encouraged to do lots of walking which I certainly did, and by now I was even starting to lift my knee as I walked to stretch the muscle groups a little more. That resulted in a very painful knee in the evening with multiple bags of frozen peas to cool it down and reduce the serious swelling.

You need a new hip

Thursday 26th June

I had another middle-of-the-night crisis, meaning I came downstairs for a read. As on the last occasion it meant I dropped back to sleep quite easily afterwards. I worried about coming down the stairs during the night with bleary eyes, but simply fidgeting on the bed was doing me no good.

Today I walked up the lane for a personal best in terms of distance of about 150metres.

The leg was getting stronger but it meant that muscles ached almost permanently, with significant swelling around the knee. As well as an ice pack I used some painkilling gel today which did appear to give some relief.

Yet another new issue came along to annoy me when I went to bed. I discovered I had a very painful right foot and I couldn't find any position to make it comfortable. Deb was having some *'me time'* watching a video before coming to bed, but when she eventually came up and found me in distress she came to my rescue. The remedy was to massage the foot for a few minutes, and instantly it felt fine again...sleep!

After a middle of the night trip to the toilet I was back in the same pain again and had to wake Deb for another massage. She was being so good to me.

You need a new hip

Friday 27ᵗʰ June

Today it was a little cooler with occasional rain, so the amount of walking in the garden I could do was limited, but I made the most of any dry spells to have a good work out.

I decided that I must have bruised the base of my right foot because of the different walking action with crutches. I couldn't stand on it for long before it throbbed. There was nothing much that could be done about it, but I decided to try and avoid thumping my foot down quite as much.

Although the swelling around the knee was reducing, I was still suffering the uncomfortable point on my buttock where the staples were really getting in the way. There were also some niggling stabbing pains around my hip area when I leant or stretched too far. The movements were all natural ones, but I had to be more careful about keeping the hip straighter.

In the evening we had a glass or two of wine as a sort of celebration of how much improvement had been possible in such a short time. I was quickly very tired and went to bed at my new normal time of 10:00 pm and fell deeply asleep until Deb arrived at about midnight. Generally we both had a much better night's sleep than before, even with my visits to the toilet every couple of hours.

You need a new hip

Saturday 28th June

Another milestone today as we went into the city for a cup of coffee. It was not pleasant being bundled into the car but a change of scenery was needed. After some thinking, I decided to sit in the back of the car where I could stretch out a little more, as well as getting in and out with less strain. I also walked further than I had done so far, getting to and from the car and the café in Debenhams. Sitting in a strange chair was a challenge, but these little trials were becoming less of a stumbling block as the days went by.

Before we came home, I sat in the car on my own while Deb went to buy a new pair of the dreaded compression socks. It was time the original ones were washed. The morning out and serious walking had really tired me out, and my heel was once again extremely uncomfortable.

Back home after nearly two hours away, Deb changed my dressing and the wound was completely dry. I decided that tomorrow I would have a shower before going to the surgery to have my staples out on Monday. Changing my compression socks was not easy as they were extremely tight and difficult for Deb to grasp while pulling them over the heel. Anyway after much 'huffing' and puffing' the first pair were off and rinsed through to be dry in case they are needed after my shower tomorrow. While the socks were being changed, Deb took the opportunity to look at the base of my foot, and as suspected there was a bruise there.

After lunch I was desperate for a rest and slept soundly on the bed for over an hour. The morning had really tired me out. I continued with my exercise regime and I was now lifting my leg much easier and certainly higher.

In a break between showers I had a walk around the garden, but my leg was really tired and aching from the morning's adventure.

On a more positive note I had been more careful about avoiding excessive twisting and stretching, and I certainly had fewer moments of the sharp pain from around the joint area.

You need a new hip

Unfortunately another issue cropped up as my eyes seemed to be very tired and I was suffering from blurred vision, both close up and far away. Looking on the internet, it seems that this does sometimes happen after anaesthesia and major surgical procedures. Luckily from the reports it appeared to be just a temporary thing, so I didn't bother my doctor about it.

Well, it was a week since coming home and I felt really quite pleased with my progress. From the weak and feeble person walking a step at a time last Saturday, and constantly looking towards the next round of painkillers, I was now walking quite quickly and confidently on my crutches and the doses of painkillers were reducing day by day.

Week Three

On Monday Deb drove me to the doctor's surgery for my appointment with the nurse to have my staples removed. I was nervous about the anticipated pain, but I needn't have worried. The nurse took no longer than ten minutes using a special extractor that simply gripped each staple and pulled it out with virtually no pain at all. She told me the wound was healing well and I no longer needed a dressing on it. The recommendation was to gently rub some cream around the area to soften the scar tissue.

Looking at the scar afterwards, we believe there were 28 of the little clips that are less than a centimetre long and just two or three millimetres deep into the flesh. I somehow thought they would be bent over at the ends like when we staple papers together, but that was a silly assumption. They just push straight into the flesh on either side of the incision and hold the area steady while the healing process begins.

I was generally becoming more mobile and quite proficient on my crutches. My walks were getting longer and faster, with fewer aches and pains afterwards. The physio exercises were also getting easier, and as well as being able to do more of them I could also extend the stretches and lift the leg far higher than before.

Without a doubt I was becoming more confident and in control of my body. This meant that Deb could spend time away from the house knowing I was safe on my own. She could take her time more doing the shopping, and even started going to her Zumba classes again. One morning while she was out I fell asleep in my chair and when I woke up there was a moment, maybe just a few seconds, when I realised I was not in any pain. That was only a fleeting moment, as the slightest movement of the leg brought discomfort initially and then pain.

There was a very positive moment this week when I had my first shower. Deb helped me into the cubicle and stood on guard throughout, but I was finally washing myself properly. It gave me such a feeling of freedom for a few minutes with warm soapy water washing away days of dirt and dead skin cells. I came out quite pleased with myself, although I tasted un-rinsed soapy residue for quite some time.

Knowing that I was able to clean myself was a major achievement, but it exhausted me and would not be repeated too often for another week or two. Of course, there was no way at that time that I could have had a shower without Deb standing nearby. I was balancing on my legs without aids during the five or ten minutes and was constantly worried about slipping.

The restrictions on bending meant that I was still unable to reach anywhere below my knees, but one morning Deb overcame a long-standing phobia she has about feet. After I had soaked my feet in a bowl of hot water she dried them gently and then cut my toe nails. I knew it was very difficult for her, but it gave me such pleasure.

I spent many hours in the garden and even made up a long length of hose pipe, that I could drag around behind me as I watered the vegetables and hanging baskets in the wonderful sunny weather we were having. The sunshine encouraged me to spend long periods outside, letting the sunshine get to my leg as we ate on the patio, or when I simply sat on my personal chair on the lawn.

On the negative side, I was still finding it impossible to sleep at night for long periods. The toilet trips continued to disturb me and it had become a regular thing to go downstairs and read a book or spend an hour on my laptop. Trying to sleep on my back was proving to be very alien to me, and my legs seemed to cry out night after night to be moved to a more comfortable position.

To add to this problem I was also too hot in bed, especially with the stupid compression socks that were now noticeably squeezing my feet. They had also become ragged, and bits of the fabric kept getting tangled around my toes, creating even more discomfort. I couldn't reach my toes yet and needed Deb to sort out the socks on a regular basis, and give my feet a short massage. This might have been acceptable during the daytime but at night I tried to avoid disturbing her. Unfortunately that just meant my feet became even more uncomfortable.

My pain was obviously reducing and that meant I was attempting to do new things. One day I felt well enough to successfully change the handle on the cloakroom door. Unfortunately it involved standing without full support for a few minutes, plus several brief moments when I twisted or leaned just a little too far. After the job was done I had to collapse in my chair again to recover.

Sadly as I was beginning to feel better I fell into the trap of trying to do things that my body wasn't quite capable of doing yet. This didn't help with my attempts to reduce the amount of painkilling pills I was taking. The wound might have been getting better but it was still giving me moments when I winced as I moved. My thigh was swollen and bruised, and there was also a nagging pain in my groin area as though something was pulling deep inside.

This shouldn't have surprised me after such an operation. The fact was that one of the biggest joints in the body had been forcefully dislocated, and then the hip end of my thigh bone sawn off, before a lump of titanium was pushed and hammered down into the remaining bone. To achieve all this, muscles in the thigh were sliced open and pulled apart to get access to the bone. Those muscles were now trying to knit together again and grow strong enough to support and move the alien lump of metal that had been added to my leg.

But the healing process was continuing, and regular creaming sessions on the scar were making the area less painful, although it was now beginning to itch.

Lack of real exercise was also making me weak, and it might have been made worse by still having to take blood-thinning pills. My walks left me puffing, and the lure of my comfortable green seat became overwhelming at times. I was positive that things were going to get better, but I was impatient to get my strength back in time to go on our world cruise in just six months' time.

More urgently we had a trip to the dentist coming up, and that would mean a long walk from the nearest car park, followed by a flight of steep stairs to go up and down on my crutches. For a bit of practice we decided to walk from home to the village pub for a drink. The locals were very surprised to see me and wished me well as I enjoyed a pint of lager before hobbling back home with a smile on my face.

It was our 39th wedding anniversary that week and we celebrated by going to a restaurant in the city for a wonderful meal. Back home again we shared a bottle of champagne while we watched one of the DVDs we had brought back from our world cruise in 2012. The memories of that adventure really encouraged me to get better so that we could repeat the experience very soon.

At the end of that third week I went to see my doctor to discuss progress. I was worried about the blurred vision. He assured me that it was nothing to do with the operation and suggested that I see my optician if I was still worried. I also mentioned the issues with my feet from the compression socks, and having seen how mobile I was he said I could now do without them. He also prescribed me a short course of gentle sleeping pills to hopefully let me have some sleep.

I left the surgery feeling so much happier.

Week Four

This week saw yet more improvements and I started to walk with just a single crutch. This made a real difference as it meant I had a hand free to carry things. On a couple of my night-time walkabouts downstairs I even took Deb a cup of tea.

The nights hadn't improved, although the sleeping pills from the doctor gave me one or two complete nights in bed, apart from trips to the toilet of course. The side effect of sleeping deeply while lying on my back was that I snored and kept Deb awake. Fortunately she didn't get angry, as she was just pleased to know I was getting a good sleep.

Trips out were getting easier as my mobility improved, and getting in and out of the car became less traumatic. We dropped in on the local Cats' Protection rehoming centre where we had been doing voluntary work, and had a chat to the staff there. They were impressed by my walking and appeared to enjoy my story. Another trip was to Hereford for our dentist appointment, but when we got there we discovered it had been cancelled without letting us know. I think they may have detected a slight annoyance from me after struggling up their staircase for nothing.

While my teeth remained unchecked I did get to the opticians for an eye test. This was an unenjoyable three quarters of an hour moving back and forth to the waiting area while I was checked in, and then subjected to the automatic test with the puffs into the eyes. Eventually I made it to the ophthalmologist for the full inspection of my eyes, and I spent several minutes fearing collisions with my leg as she constantly wandered around menacingly close to my leg. Anyway I did need new glasses, but the change was quite small so panic over.

I was now taking showers without Deb as a bodyguard. My balance and agility was rapidly improving so I could enjoy longer and more relaxed showers at last.

You need a new hip

Of course the better I felt the more I wanted to do, and I began to look at the jobs that needed doing all over the house and in the garden. I was nowhere near able enough to do most of the things on my list, but there were some victories.

In the garden I finally managed to do some work. Digging was banned for nine months, but I was able to prepare an area where the rhubarb was moving to. This was a slow job and involved Deb digging a barrowful of the rough soil from the patch, and then I sat with a sieve and carefully broke it up before returning it to the patch. I could only do a little at a time, and the job actually took several days to complete an area ready for just four rhubarb plants.

The weather continued to be glorious on most days but this meant the lawn needed cutting and Deb was in charge of the lawnmower for a week or two yet. I was only able to sit and watch her and became more and more frustrated with my inability to do the things that were normally my responsibility. At least I could water the plants.

Late one afternoon while sitting on my chair allowing the sun to get to my legs, I noticed that my right foot was swollen. There was no obvious reason, and no pain, but it felt tight. I decided to lie on the bed and keep my foot raised for half an hour. It didn't make the swelling go down but at least it relaxed a little. After dinner I sat with the foot in a bowl of cold water for half an hour, and it was really soothing, but the swelling remained the same. This was worrying, as I was panicking that it might be a blood clot.

As the evening progressed I became more and more worried and rang the out-of-normal-hours emergency health service number. After explaining about the hip replacement and this sudden problem with my foot, Deb took me to the hospital. We waited for over an hour before a doctor looked and prodded my foot. He was happy that there was no blood clot and suspected there might just be some bruising. More than two hours after I made the call we were home again, with no idea of what

You need a new hip

was causing my swollen foot, but much happier that there was nothing seriously wrong.

With that panic over we got to bed rather late that night, and I had a reasonable sleep – give or take a couple of semi-conscious trots to the toilet.

The following evening we had been invited for a barbecue at our neighbours' house. Several other people were there and we had some lovely food and the chat became loud and amusing as the excess of wine and cider loosened our tongues. I had consumed more alcohol that evening than for several weeks and slept rather well.

Lunchtime that day brought another small victory. So far while at the dining table I had had to pull the chair back before sitting down and then dragging the table back over my legs. But that day I succeeded in sitting down and taking my weight sufficiently to pull the chair in behind me and under the table.

Yes I know...BIG DEAL!

Good point, but it was quite satisfying to me.

My exercises continued to go well: my leg looked less wasted and the loose skin behind my knee was beginning to tighten up again. Walking was easy and I even tried to change my stair climbing technique. So far I had been taking a step up with the good leg before bringing the injured one to the same step. Now I was achieving one or two steps where I led with the injured leg. I couldn't do very many steps like this, but it forced the leg muscles to get used to some different actions again.

Against all the recommendations I even took a few paces around the house without any crutches. These few simple steps might have been slow and tentative but I managed it without causing any pain.

You need a new hip

While on the subject of pain, this fourth week was also the moment when I realised that I was no longer feeling the pain that I suffered from before the operation.

Things were looking so much better.

I hate nights

This may seem overly melodramatic but this was a time when I dreaded going to bed at night.

So far there had been thirty uncomfortable, sometimes painful nights of sleeping on my back with no chance of lying on my side, or with my legs bent. My best nights had produced perhaps four to five hours sleep, but just as likely it had been two to three hours.

I typically went to bed at about 11:00 pm, and being exhausted I fell asleep almost instantly. It was rarely later than 12:45 am before I was awake again. After fidgeting for maybe an hour trying to get comfortable, I would feel guilty for disturbing Deb, so I'd hobble my way downstairs to read until I felt tired again.

An hour later I could be back in bed confident of getting some sleep, and I probably would nod off for a while, but usually before 3:00 am I would be wide awake again. This was a period of the recovery when my foot would scream at me to allow it to move. After a toilet trot I'd stare up at the ceiling in the dark hoping for dreams, but I'd have no option but to gently flex my feet, or repeatedly straighten and bend my legs. These exercises were sometimes successful enough to fool my muscles and allow the '*go to sleep*' messages from my brain to be accepted.

On the worst nights I would be downstairs by 4:30 am and reading once more. Sometimes I had a cup of tea and even occasionally a bowl of cereal to try to kid my aching legs that it was daytime, when I usually got very tired. By the time I got back to bed again it would be daylight. Sometimes I slept but there were many mornings when I would be up yet again by 7:00 am to make us both a cup of tea and take my pills before Deb would get up and bring me some breakfast.

Now I would want to sleep.

You need a new hip

Before I even had the operation I knew it would be difficult sleeping on my back, but I assumed that eventually exhaustion would force my body and brain to accept this new sleeping position. Well, in my case it didn't.

I struggled to relax with the heat that seemed to surround my body, and no chance to move and find a cool spot. The pillows were another source of heat, and my head searched for any tiny spot of cool area within its small arc of possible movement. With my legs restricted to the same position for several hours they yearned for movement that was impossible. Even when I did achieve a few minutes of deep sleep, I would snore and that gave me a sore throat, plus a desperate need for a drink.

There was still another twenty or so days before I was to see the consultant who would hopefully give me the all-clear to return to my natural sleeping habits. I knew that I wasn't ready for that change of position quite yet, as even the slightest accidental pressure to the side of the wound brought me pain.

I was obviously getting better, and was confident that very soon I would appreciate the new hip giving me back the freedom of painless movement. But nights were a nightmare and sometimes my bed felt like a prison.

Five Weeks Gone

Yes, five weeks had gone by since 'hip day' and the time was dragging until I got the all-clear to return to normal sleeping positions, crossing my legs perhaps, and bending down to touch my right foot.

The foot continued to hurt almost daily, so I intended to ask the surgeon (when I saw him) if anything he had done could have caused my discomfort. In the meantime I took to wearing a sock on the offending foot to protect it a little while I walked.

Apart from boredom of seeing jobs that needed to be done, and not being able to do anything about them, my life was going well. My 63rd birthday was coming up and, ignoring my hip, I still feel much younger since retirement.

During this week I managed to reduce my painkilling pills down to half the maximum dose, so progress was being made. I still had pain, but not as intense as it had been, and the more exercises I did the better it seemed to be getting. During this week I also took the final blood-thinning pill, so quite a positive week from the drug perspective.

One month after the operation and everything seemed to be going well except for sleeping. I hardly slept for more than a couple of hours at a time, so ended up walking around the house at night and acting like a zombie during the day.

We finally managed to see our dentist and both of us came away with no treatment needed. Just like at the opticians, I felt very vulnerable sitting in the treatment chair while the dentist came very near to my leg. I should have been able to trust these professionals but I couldn't.

Deb and I reluctantly agreed to try some drastic action and against everything I hold dear, we slept in separate rooms. The idea was to give Deb a chance of getting more sleep, and me a chance to feel less restricted about getting up during the night. That first night, even with a thunderstorm rumbling outside, I slept better than I had done for some time, and it was 8:00 am when I finally woke. It seemed to have been a good idea, but only as temporary measure.

My major accomplishment for the week was feeling good enough to mow the lawn. Deb kept an eye on me, but I slowly managed to cut most of the grass before I became exhausted. Poor Deb then had to finish to job while I rested with my leg raised up.

Yes, I was tired and sore after the effort, but it was worth a little bit of pain to take another step back towards normality again.

The second night sleeping on my own was not so successful, but rather than getting up and wandering around the house, I was able to lie there and read my book. This meant I could simply turn the light off and go to sleep when my eyes became too heavy to read any more.

After three nights on my own I returned to our shared bed. I didn't enjoy being alone, and accepted that if I couldn't sleep then I had to get up and go downstairs for a read. It was another disturbed night, and the temptation to roll onto my side was getting stronger.

There were hopefully only another couple of weeks to wait.

One morning while Deb went shopping (to get my birthday present) I had a go at repairing the roller blind covering the garage window. This meant standing on a step ladder which was another first. The repairs allowed me to close the blind while I was having my shower rather than expose myself to anyone wandering into our garden.

As a little experiment I even tried sitting on the toilet without my throne, and successfully managed to sit and get up without any discomfort. I wasn't ready to completely do without my throne quite yet but knew it wouldn't be long.

I also continued to have a few minutes walking with no crutches when I moved around the house. It wasn't causing me any pain, but I was very careful not to try and do too much at once. Walking longer distances (with the crutch) was really improving, and Deb and I planned to have a go at walking all the way around the village in the next few days.

Out in the garden I managed to kneel down with my dodgy leg stretched out behind me while I did some weeding. This rather clumsy looking pose was the recommended way of getting down to ground level. It allowed me to clear a patch of weeds, but the different position and muscles involved made my leg ache afterwards.

As with all my experiments while recovering my mobility, I worried that I was trying to do too much and too soon.

The Six-Week Milestone

I was at the six week mark where, according to the information I was given, I would be able to do things that hadn't been possible so far.

The booklet I was given in the hospital suggested several things were now possible. I could start some new light exercise such as swimming, gentle jogging, and cycling. I was even allowed to start dancing again. There was a chance I could drive once more, but I decided to delay a decision on that until I saw the surgeon in a week's time.

The most significant change possible was that I was allowed to sleep on my side, so I spent quite a time looking on the internet for advice on how to support the leg with pillows and possibly try it out.

Yippee!

Sadly there seemed to be total confusion about this subject on the internet. Some medical sites said 12 weeks was the earliest date for lying on my side. Others supported my own information, but again with differing recommendations. Some said I must lie on my uninjured side while others said it could only be on the injured side. There was general agreement that there must be serious amounts of pillows between the legs to avoid getting the dodgy leg in the wrong place.

What I did discover was that I should have been exercising my leg while lying down and lifting it up sideways. That hadn't been pointed out to me by the hospital physiotherapist. Anyway, I had a go at it, and it was now added to my list of physical workouts.

Another major landmark was that I could throw away my crutches, and I was quite happy with that idea, although I continued to keep one near to hand, for when I felt tired.

You need a new hip

Well, a combination of trying new things, and the excitement of seeing my family on my birthday pushed my body to the limit. No matter how much I tried to be careful, I desperately wanted to be fit and active again.

When our grandson was here I spent too long holding him and walking around with him in my arms.

Out in the garden I spent too long working with my leg stretched behind me, and my experiments to improve walking up and down stairs were just too much.

My leg ached seriously and it felt as if it was deep inside around the hip joint.

A WARNING

This is for anyone who is following my story and is in a similar or imminent state of hip replacement.

Don't try and do too much.

Many of the things I did were attempted before they should have been. There were several moments when I knew I had done too much or done something that I shouldn't have even considered. The result was an increase in the pain, and although I know muscles hurt as they are encouraged to do more, sometimes the pain didn't feel as if it was coming from my muscles. I just hoped that my short term efforts hadn't done anything that could affect my long term recovery.

If you try something new as you recover, do it gently and stop if there is even a hint of discomfort. Have a rest for a few hours from that activity, and then try it again and see if it gets easier. If it does then perhaps you can do it a little more, but if it still hurts, **DON'T DO IT!!**

So, this is just a warning for you all.

Things get easier day by day, but just because a new position, or a new movement didn't hurt immediately, don't think you can be an Olympic champion in that discipline. The new joint is a valuable piece of metalwork that has been attached to your body, and pain from a bad activity might take a while to manifest itself.

BE CAREFUL!

Almost time to see the surgeon again

It was the seventh week since my operation and very soon I would be seeing Mr Oakley at the hospital again to review my progress.

This was a period when my recovery was really moving forward quite spectacularly, with the crutches almost forgotten and my leg was becoming less and less painful as I became ever more mobile. A slight issue was that as I was now walking unaided, my left knee was aching. This knee had been in trouble for many years and seemed to be suggesting that it also needed some attention.

As I was feeling so much better, Deb booked us a weekend break. It was at a rather nice country hotel about an hour away, on the outskirts of Chepstow. It had a swimming pool and a health spa to give us a chance of some pampering, and a break for Deb from cooking and cleaning while I lazed my days away.

I was now attempting to spend a few minutes each night on my side, but the wound was still very sore when I lay on it. Turning the other way seemed more comfortable but I was not sure I should be doing it.

The raised toilet seat had been removed as I felt quite happy sitting and getting up from the normal-height seat. I also had to be sure I could do without it when we went to the hotel. I was definitely not taking the plastic throne with us.

My next target was to have a bath.

One day I got into the empty bath and checked that I could carefully lie down without any discomfort. Then slowly and gently I managed to stand up and get out without any need for help. My only issue was that I couldn't lean forward enough to turn taps on or off without bending too much.

You need a new hip

The intention was to try it out at the hotel where the bath might be bigger, but I couldn't resist the idea and gave in to a hot, deep, and bubbly bath a couple of evenings later. It was superb and I discovered that once in the bath I could turn the taps off with my toes.

In terms of pain I was now going through a new phase where muscles were beginning to recover and the discomfort I was most regularly feeling was in my groin area.

Oh, and plus my knees of course.

On Sunday 3rd August it was time to start our break. We packed our bags with one small one each so that I could do a bit and carry my own case. Mine had a vast stock of pills, creams and 'just in case' supports as well as a few clothes and washing kit. There was some light-hearted banter that I needed a seriously bigger case than Deb.

The journey was uncomfortable, especially as I had now returned to the front passenger seat. Fortunately the drive was only an hour, so we soon getting out at the beautiful hotel. Once unpacked, we went straight to the swimming pool where Deb enjoyed a good work out while I gently managed just six lengths of the 15-metre pool. By the end of that I was aching and puffed out. I realised just how unfit I had become.

My leg was stiff for the rest of the afternoon and evening but I was extremely happy to have swum again.

The next morning we walked around Chepstow for nearly three hours and I had to resort to the walking stick to give my leg a bit of a rest. We had bought the stick a few weeks earlier as a *'just in case'* item and this was its first outing.

When we got back to the hotel it was swimming time again, and I managed eight lengths plus a lot of kicking at the end of the pool. I felt rather proud with my efforts and I was certainly not as shattered as yesterday.

You need a new hip

I may not have felt bad straight after the swim but an hour later my leg was oh so stiff. I wasn't overly concerned as the ache was most definitely muscle based, and I knew my thigh muscles needed a lot of building up after weeks of inactivity.

After a second night of relaxation it was time to go home. The morning was damp so we didn't stop anywhere on the homeward journey, and hence I was extremely stiff again by the time I crawled out of the car an hour later.

The rest of my day was sedentary. I was aching, and the weather was not encouraging me to do anything physical. Swimming had certainly given my leg a thorough testing and I enjoyed it, but wow it made me tired.

When I had finished my bath (yes, another one) I checked my weight. I had put on 5 lbs since the operation. Not really surprising considering I normally use a lot of energy working and digging in the garden. I decided to cut back on the food and get my body back to where I feel comfortable.

Having been away for a couple of days we had to go shopping, and this was the first time I had pushed a supermarket trolley since the operation. You might think the trolley would be easy as it is like using a walking aid, but they are tricky to steer around the end of the aisles and it puts sideways strain on the hip joint. At least I felt confident enough to do it again.

In case you are wondering if my nights were getting better, I am afraid not. Occasional sleeps on my side might make me a little happier, but sleep was still hard to achieve and certainly not for long periods.

I really did hope the sleep soon improved and I could feel less tired during the day again.

Time for a review with my surgeon

Seven weeks had passed since my operation and things were generally going very well. I had no worries as Deb and I went back to the hospital on Thursday 7th July for a mid-morning appointment with my surgeon.

We arrived early in the hope of getting seen quickly, but just as we sat in the waiting area the nurse came out of her hiding place to warn people that Mr Oakley was running nearly an hour late.

Amazingly just five minutes later I was called in to the consulting room.

Mr Oakley swept in to the cubicle and asked a few questions about how I was. I told him that I felt well and the only niggles were the pain in my groin and the area of the scar. He took notes and didn't give any answers. After a look at my scar he said it was looking fine, and then sent me for an x-ray. When I got back from my photographic session, the nurse appeared again to warn the waiting crowd that there was now a delay of an hour and a quarter.

Deb decided to go and move the car, as the parking ticket was running out.

Eventually I was called back in to see my overworked consultant. He was happy with my x-ray and showed me where the bone was growing over the metalwork of my artificial hip. I was told to walk as much as I could and to be careful not to jump around or fall over for three months to avoid damaging my new hip. These instructions were also enhanced by a request to be careful for a while longer to avoid damaging his statistics for the operation. He has a good success record for hip replacements, and wants to keep it.

The rest of my time slot allowed me to ask the usual questions of what I could and couldn't do. Mr Oakley was very positive, and although I needed to be sensible for another three months I could now mow the

You need a new hip

lawn carefully and at night I could lie on the operated leg side, but not the other one.

Whoops!

Finally he gave me the all clear to start driving again and said he wanted to see me again in twelve months' time.

I was very happy with the outcome of the meeting, and smiling when I returned to Deb in the waiting room. On the way out of the hospital, we took the crutches back to the physiotherapy department, and a few minutes later we were on our way home. I didn't drive, as I had been man-handled a bit and wasn't totally ready to take over the steering wheel quite yet.

Of course I had totally forgotten to push Mr Oakley about my painful groin and scar. I assumed that these minor issues were typical at seven weeks and didn't require any comment from the expert.

So after nearly two and a half years, two hospitals, two surgeons and various injections and scans, I was on the road to recovery. By the time we went on the world cruise in January I should be fit and pain-free with all the hopes of an enjoyable and active three month adventure.

For the rest of the summer I continued to get stronger and more active. My leg became less painful, although I still suffered with occasional bouts of pain around the area of the wound and in my groin. However I had to put this into perspective as what I was now feeling was nothing in comparison to how I felt for the first couple of weeks after the operation. The activities I was doing made my muscles ache, but that was expected as I got my legs back into a decent condition again. My knees were a bit of a problem but they had been for many years, and Mr Oakley had said that I should see my GP if they remained bad and I could go on a list again for more surgery.

Umm!

You need a new hip

The really positive thing was that I didn't have the feeling in my hip that I had before the operation. There was no pain when I turned on my leg, and I didn't have the feeling that the hip might collapse anymore. It looked as if the operation had been a success, even if it did take far longer to happen than it perhaps should have done.

Doubts set in

The NHS is rather slow sometimes but they do a fantastic job. Having been told by Mr Oakley that everything was going well and there was no need to see him again for a year, I accepted his word. I assumed that the niggling little aches in my groin and around the scar were normal and would get better with time.

After all, it was amazingly better than before the replacement.

As the summer days of 2014 shortened and autumn took over, I was mobile, reasonably pain-free, and sleeping almost as well as I used to.

Few people would have realised that I had received a new hip. I walked normally, and was able to do most things quite naturally again. I was happy, and the months of pain before the operation were just a distant memory.

I had spoken to several people who had received new hips, or knees, or both. My recovery appeared similar to others though there were some people who expressed shock at how well I was doing, while others scoffed that they couldn't believe how long my recovery was taking.

My belief is that different people have different expectations from a new hip. Many are in such severe pain before they receive their artificial joint that they are so happy to find themselves reasonably free of that pain, and able to move around independently. There are others who have a different view, and expect more. Perhaps they are still working, or have had a really active life, or might even have a lower pain threshold.

I am one of those people, and we will do everything possible to convince the NHS that we need our joint replacing sooner than our consultant considers it necessary. The drawback with this scenario is that we may recall more recent memories of being truly active, and want to return quickly to that state.

You need a new hip

So as the leaves began turning to their autumn colours I became slightly frustrated that my progress appeared to have plateaued. Yes, I could move quite freely, but I still had discomfort that didn't seem to be improving no matter how much exercise I took. Getting in and out of the car was a matter of swinging my legs rather than just a natural movement, and I still winced a little as I sat down or stood up. The wound area itched after exercise, and my groin area continued to be painful at times.

Was this as good as it was going to get?

We reached another milestone in October when it was time to pay the balance of our fares for the world cruise. I just didn't feel confident enough to go ahead with it, and Deb and I took the sad decision to ring P&O and postpone our adventure for a year. I was continually asking myself if the ache in the groin and the occasional pain around the area of the scar would ever go away. Painkillers were still needed, and although I was quite active there didn't seem to be any new improvements or achievements like there had been for the first two or three months.

Eventually I booked an appointment with my GP and politely asked if this was the best I could anticipate. He was genuinely surprised that I was still having issues. Before going to the drastic action of sending me back to the consultant, he decided to get me an appointment with the practice's physiotherapist.

Wow!

A month later I trotted into a consulting room to see an enthusiastic young physiotherapist.

While he was looking at my notes he asked me to explain my history and what problems I was still having. I then had to stand and perform a series of movements to show how much I could bend and stretch the leg. Then he made me lie on a couch and proceeded to prod my leg while moving it in various directions.

More exercises now, starting with some while lying flat on my back. First I had to bend the affected leg at the knee and pull it up as tight as I could towards my stomach. Next with my good leg kept straight, I drew the other foot up until it lay next to my good knee with the knee pointing up to the ceiling. Now he asked me to allow the knee to fall outwards (without moving my foot) and try to get the knee as close to the bed as I could.

My young physiotherapist was not impressed and *"tutted"* at my efforts. My notes suggested I had a perfectly good hip joint but I was not able to move it as much as I should have been able to, and my leg flexibility was poor.

In my defence, the only instruction I had been given by the surgeon was to walk a lot, and be careful not to fall over. There had been no suggestions as to what I could do to improve the mobility, and more importantly, no mention of just how far my joint could be bent. Sadly I had been keeping movement to a minimum in the belief that walking was sufficient to complete the healing process.

Oh boy was I wrong!!

The physiotherapist, who specialised in sports injuries, told me to repeat the two exercises on my back several times a day. I also had to stretch out the thigh muscles and to do this I was to stand and take a pace forward with my good leg. Then I had to straighten the dodgy leg behind me and push my body weight forward and over the good leg.

He then discussed my walking. Most people may walk long distances but do it gently. Our paces don't go forwards very far and, more importantly, we don't extend the foot behind us. I was now instructed to walk far more athletically and to push the trailing leg and foot as far as possible behind me at the end of each step. This makes the steps much longer and makes the leg muscles work far harder.

Finally he came to the most confusing bit. I had to get control of, and work my pelvic floor muscles. Now most women will understand this as something important after childbirth, but to me (and possibly many men) it means nothing. So his instructions were to *"pull everything in"*. That meant clenching my stomach muscles, and those in my backside, plus those muscles that are used to stop ourselves passing water. This made me think for a while as it was something I had never considered, or attempted before. Anyway, my homework instructions were to try my exercises, and power-walking, while holding the pelvic floor muscles tight.

During the forty five minute session I became slightly disappointed that I had not been told to exercise like this before. At the same time I was also more positive that things could be improved. An appointment was made for the following week and I made my way home. Of course I did what I had been told to do, and probably looked quite ridiculous as I stretched my legs out while walking at the same time as holding my pelvic muscles tight. The effort and confusion caused by my attempts to 'hold myself in' initially made me hold my breath and contort my face.

Then I realised I was being followed.

As if my contortions had all been due to a temporary attack of cramp, I stopped and allowed the person to quickly pass by me while I rubbed my leg.

You need a new hip

When I got home I explained what I was told and showed Deb the exercises. She chuckled about the pelvic floor muscles and over the next few days I was the laughing stock of all our friends.

Just 24 hours later I was virtually pain free. I succeeded in touching the underneath of my foot on the injured leg for the first time since the operation, and I put my sock on without having to support the foot on the bed and groan.

A week later and I was walking properly and noticeably extending my thigh muscles with each step. I was able to have a bath without supporting the foot on the end of the bath. To put it simply, I was feeling positive and really felt that I had a new hip at last.

On my second visit to my physio guru, he was pleased to see and hear the results of my efforts and gave me further torturous exercises to do for a few weeks. This time I had to work on my thigh muscles.

The first exercise consisted of standing with one leg forward half a pace, and the other slightly back. I had to bend my front knee and drop my body down, then bring my body up again. This had to be done for each leg and would strengthen muscles in the upper leg and knee area.

Secondly, I had to stand on one leg, and while supporting myself by resting my hand on a chair, I should allow the knee to bend and then straighten it again.

Finally, there was a new lying-down exercise. While on my good side I had to slide both knees up in front of me to about a right angle. Then I had to raise my bad knee up while my foot stayed still. This stretched the muscles on the inside of the thigh, and more importantly those around my groin.

That was more than enough to be going on with until I would see my ever-smiling physiotherapist again after Christmas.

Before I left that day I suggested that all hip replacement patients should have access to this physiotherapy, but his answer shocked me. Although a lot of people would benefit from the physiotherapy some don't need it, or don't realise they need it. Appointments are only offered when people express concern to their GP that things are not going as well as they expected. If everyone was to be offered consultations automatically, there wouldn't be enough physiotherapists, or money in the budget, to provide the service. Accepting his views I realised I should have complained to my doctor earlier.

Anyway, I continued with the exercises although some proved very difficult. I am sure the one legged knee dips were doing me good, but they really hurt the knees. Alongside the workouts I was also massaging cream into the scar to soften the tissues and encourage the healing process.

By the time I went back to the physiotherapist just after Christmas 2014 there had been many improvements and I can truly say that having the hip replacement had worked for me. I was bending down and touching my toes, I was doing sit-ups and even kneeling down and getting up on each leg without support.

The changes in just a few weeks had been amazing!!

That was my final visit to the young man who had achieved so much. There was little or no massage or manipulation; he just showed me a series of exercises that would make my hip more agile and improve the muscle tone in my legs. He allowed me to realise what my hip was capable of doing, and then helped me to actually do it.

Winter 2014

There was a less dramatic period of recovery during the winter months. Walking was less appealing, although we did get out as much as ppossible when it was dry. Nothing much could be done in the garden because it was mainly muddy patches where vegetables had been. My slightly under-par ability to dig in the garden led us to buy a motorised cultivator to help me get the ground ready for winter. This meant I could make the most of any dry days while avoiding the long periods of digging that really made my muscles ache. I also took the opportunity to get out there and chop logs for our fire whenever I could, and that was another activity that gave my thigh a significant test.

Indoors there were various DIY projects to be started and completed. We had builders in to carry out some major changes to wall layouts, enabling me to bring the shower in from the garage and reposition it in the newly-extended downstairs cloakroom. Unfortunately the expensive shower cubicle bought before the operation was too big for the new space, and we had to buy another. Over the weeks of cold and wet weather I managed to make quite a good job of it, and the new shower was ready for use before the winter ended. Between us we completed all the planned downstairs decorating, so we decided to have a break before we started on the upstairs rooms of the house.

My aches and pains were infinitely better than before the physiotherapy, and I was able to be more energetic in my movements. The DIY work involved a lot of lifting, and working on step-ladders, and that made my leg suffer at times. I had moments when I worried that I had done too much, but usually a couple of days of lighter activities eased the aches. My thigh muscles were being used far more, and beginning to recover some of the tone (and bulk) that was lost when large chunks of my tissues were cut apart to allow access to the hip joint. There was a simple way of knowing when I had pushed the muscles further than I should have because the scar area itched. I often resorted to rubbing the scar to get relief, but if Deb noticed, she would gently remind me to take a rest.

The exercises I had been shown continued, but I became bored with some of them, and those that required me to take weight on my knees were proving far too painful to do often. If I did push myself too far with these particular workouts it took several days before my knees recovered, and I had to balance the potential benefits to the hip, against the possible damage I was doing to my knees. I constantly experimented to find an exercise that flexed different muscles in the weakened area of my thigh, as I was very aware that the wound still had significant patches where muscles just hadn't regrown. Perhaps they never will, but I do remember that the physiotherapist had said that it would take up to 18 months before I could expect a full recovery.

Deb and I took a short break in Cornwall during January. The weather completely surprised us with a warm and sunny couple of days while we visited my brothers and looked around the area we know so well. That short spell of good weather was a rare treat, and there were many weeks of cool and damp weather to come yet before we would have the warmth of summer.

I decided it was time to give dancing a try again. A quick search on the internet identified a dancing school in Hereford and after a phone call we joined and began a weekly class to get back into the swing of ballroom dancing. It was a beginner's class that we knew would be going over much that we had done before, but it was all about going through the moves again to see how it affected me. So every Wednesday we had an hour of waltz, quickstep, and foxtrot, and it was wonderful to be making our way around a dancefloor again, even if it was a little tiring with lots of repetition of certain steps and movements.

There were times when my leg quietly told me off if the steps involved a lot of twisting, and I came away most evenings feeling tired, but we were slowly growing more confident as the memories of what we had learnt before came back.

You need a new hip

Several months previously we had booked a cruise for the end of June which was going across the Mediterranean to Venice, and which coincided with the date of our Ruby wedding anniversary. As we waited for the summer to arrive we got itchy feet again so I booked a week's coach break to southern Ireland for the end of April. Just like the surprisingly warm weather we had in Cornwall, our visit to Ireland coincided with a delightful few days of sunshine, and turned out to be rather special. With some wonderful countryside plus a lovely hotel it opened our eyes to Ireland's beauty and relaxed way of life. Unfortunately the long periods of sitting in a coach didn't do my leg much good, and we weren't sure if coach travel was the right thing at this stage in my recovery.

When we got back from Ireland it was time for some serious work in the garden. A small area already had onions and a row of early potatoes growing, but now it was time to finish the vegetable patch. This tested the leg to extremes, and I had more and more moments of the itchy wound and quite serious discomfort. Once again I recognised when I had done too much, and gave myself a day or two off to recover.

The weekly dancing lesson continued and eventually we spent an evening at a social dance organised by the school. For nearly three hours we waltzed and quickstepped, as well as doing the occasional sequence dance that we had mastered. It felt good, and it gave my confidence a boost that I was able to do virtually anything I wanted to again.

Looking back I am not sure I expected to be ready to dance again so soon, or do quite as much DIY in the house, or complete so much in the garden. I certainly felt that I had achieved a great deal in less than nine months. Of course, I'd almost forgotten the two or three years before the operation; the pains that I lived with had gone, and any discomfort I was feeling now was usually a part of the recovery process.

Little achievements continued to happen over the months. Just putting socks on while standing was a major improvement, and being able to inspect the bottom of my foot was marvellous, especially as that soon led to massaging and scratching it without having to hold my breath. One simple pleasure was being able to cross my legs without pain, but it took weeks to build up the muscle just to lift my leg high enough.

I suppose the most difficult challenge left is to move quickly. I still haven't got the confidence to make sudden movements with my leg, but the muscle is getting stronger and I have jogged for a little way without mishap or pain. It is amazing that even after such a long time I still doubt the strength of the artificial ball and socket, and fear it might dislocate or fall to bits. Sadly even having researched and discovered that there are thousands of successful hip replacements annually, I continue to doubt that man can better nature's own materials.

I am sure I will trust it one day.

Summer 2015

At the end of June to celebrate my new hip's first birthday, we packed our mountain of suitcases and made our way to Southampton to have 17 days on board P&O's *Arcadia* for a cruise across the Mediterranean to Venice, plus several other wonderful ports. The early weeks of summer 2015 in Britain had not been the sunniest, but that cruise turned out to be almost constant blue skies and high temperatures. We met some lovely people on the ship and had several enjoyable hours on the dance floor. Thoughts of gardening and DIY were forgotten, and my legs were virtually pain free.

One day at breakfast we chatted with a couple and the lady had also recently received a new hip. Sadly we bored our spouses for several minutes while we talked operations and titanium implants. Surprisingly, we discovered that we had both suffered from a sore foot after the replacement.

It made me wonder just how common this problem is?

On 5th July we were in Corfu and it was hot and sunny just like our wedding day exactly 40 years before. We had a wonderful Ruby Wedding Anniversary walk around the town in the morning before just enjoying the sunshine in the afternoon. That was followed by dinner in one of the superb restaurants on the ship with a bottle of pink champagne to wash it down. I was pain free and enjoying my life again.

This cruise was the longest one we had been on for three years, and we enjoyed every moment of it. Sadly it had to end, but I had another major landmark just around the corner when I would be having a review of my recovery at the hospital again.

Just after lunch on Thursday 30th July 2015 we were walking into Hereford Hospital for my progress check. As usual we arrived early in the hope of getting an early slot, and we were the first to take our seats in the out-patient fracture clinic waiting area. As expected the nurse called me within five minutes to go for an x-ray. Here things were not quite as quick, and there was a 30-minute wait before I got the latest pictures of my hip taken. Back at the fracture clinic I re-joined Deb and noticed a sign saying that Mr Oakley was not in that afternoon. So it was going to be a registrar giving me the news about my x-ray, plus a once-over of my progress. It was a surprisingly quiet clinic, and I only had to wait for about ten minutes for the call to a cubicle.

I don't remember the surgeon's name and I hadn't seen him before. I waited as he looked at my notes and then inspected my x-ray. Prompted by the usual *"how is it going"* question I said I was still having pain in my groin as well as the aches from the leg muscles and itching around the wound area. As usual my comments appeared to be ignored, and he told me that the x-ray showed a perfect joint and the shadow seen 12 months earlier had now gone.

What shadow?

Anyway he continued by pointing out two little grey bits on the screen that he nonchalantly referred to with a Latin term. Apparently they were little bits of bone that could be pressing on my wound and might be why I get the itch. Without a chance to take this in and think about it, he said that everything appeared good and I should be able to do everything normally. The high speed consultation was coming to an end but I still complained that my knee was giving me trouble. He looked at the two-year-old x-ray and said it looked fine but I might need a scan if it got any worse.

This was how things started with my hip issues, and once again any previous findings from my investigations in Staffordshire were being ignored. To save him the trouble I made it clear that there was no way I was going to progress the knee problems now as I was going on the world cruise in six months' time. That brought a smile of satisfaction on his face knowing that he didn't have to make any further decisions or referrals.

You need a new hip

My time with him was over, and he said that I didn't need any further checks unless I get a problem. With hands shaken I was politely shown the way out and I walked away still wondering why my groin ached, and now had extra concerns about fragments of bone floating around my thigh.

At least I knew the replacement procedure had been successful and I have a joint that should last me many years. There was no ongoing medical issue to hamper the world cruise in January 2016. The niggling groin discomfort must just be something that will go away with time, and I possibly have a reason for my wound itch.

I gave the good news to Deb and we were on our way home in little more than an hour after we had arrived.

And that was it. In just over thirteen months my replacement hip was deemed a success and my life could continue as if nothing had happened.

Could this really be the end?

Coming up to date

It is now the end of August 2015 and the rather disappointing summer seems to be coming to an end. There is less than five months until we set off on our cruise to miss the worst of the winter. We have a lot to do in those five months.

As well as fitting in visits to spend some time with the family we have to sort out visas and any vaccinations necessary, plus travel arrangements to and from the cruise terminal in Southampton and a hotel for the night before we leave. I need some new summer clothes to replace my well-worn wardrobe, and I have finally convinced Deb to look at new formal dresses.

In the meantime (I hear you ask) how is my leg?

Well I really am so very pleased with it. Yes I continue to ache after working hard in the garden and my thigh still has an obvious scar plus quite an ugly area where the muscle has not regrown. The positive things are that I can walk as far as I want, DIY is possible again, and gardening is getting back to normal. And I have even played with the football that our neighbour gave me. When our grandson comes to visit he loves to run after the ball and kick or throw it around. I show typical grandad skills retrieving it from under hedges as well as playing 'keepy up' to impress him.

That moment when my troubles all started with a game of cricket plus that stupid dance on the ship, was almost three and a half years ago. When told that my suspected hernia was actually a worn out hip I thought my life would never be the same again. The long drawn out series of hospital visits where I was poked and prodded, had scans and pain-killing injections finally resulted in having quite a sizable operation. I have cost the National Health Service serious money, and tied up the valuable resources of two health authorities, but it seems to have been a success.

You need a new hip

The most dramatic result is that the pain I experienced for over two years has gone. In fact I find it difficult to remember just how bad it was, unless I read the notes I kept of the days and nights when I was close to tears with the never-ending pain.

Of course the operation produced new and different aches and pains caused by the immensity of the procedure that the surgeons performed. I remember a surgeon explaining the operation to Frank, who was in the bed next to me in the hospital, after he asked why he was in so much pain.

The response was quite stark.

"Of course it's going to hurt. We have just sliced open one of the biggest muscles in your body. Then we broke one of the biggest bones in your body and dislocated one of the biggest joints in your body".

I had researched the operation long before I eventually lay on the operating table and had a pretty good idea of what was involved, and accepted it was going to be painful. That response from the surgeon just confirmed what my body had been through.

There was an initial pain free period for a few hours the evening of my operation while I was still under the influence of the chemicals in my body, but once they had been rinsed out of my system, I struggled with the sickening agony in my hip and thigh. The nurses did their best to keep me dosed with painkilling drugs, but like hundreds of others I had been taking stronger and stronger pills for many months, and it was a struggle to give my body any relief. The discomfort was made worse by tasteless food and a lack of sleep while lying on my back being serenaded by a chorus of snorers and squeaky trolleys through the very hot nights.

Another memory on the first day after the operation was when the nurse asked me to move my leg. My brain sent the correct message, and I made the appropriate effort to lift my leg from the bed, but absolutely nothing happened. There must have been fear written across my face as the nurse immediately told me to relax and not to worry as it takes a time for the muscles to react after the operation. I repeated my attempts in the hours that followed, and little by little I noticed a feeling of movement and then my leg finally began to rise.

From simple movement I was soon being coaxed to stand with a frame, and just like thousands of other people, I was terrified as I took the weight on that leg for the first time. Despite my concerns, the shaft of titanium didn't break. Once convinced that this new hip was as strong as the old one, I began to move gingerly and within 48 hours I was walking with crutches without a safety net. Although I was noticeably getting control of my body again, the lack of home comforts, boredom and sleepless nights made those first three days in hospital worse than I could have ever imagined, and the relief of getting home was as good as any morphine pills or injections I had been given.

With the help of Deb plus an eagerness to regain control of my body, the first few weeks of my recovery brought new victories almost every day. I stood longer, walked further, and walked quicker as confidence and strength returned. The biggest issue was sleeping while lying on my back, and to be honest I never overcame that problem. For those first six weeks night-time was a torture, and it was such a relief when I was able to turn on to my side, even if that brought further pain.

While on the subject of pain, those painkillers that I had been devouring like sweets were still vital for a long time, but eventually my dependency on them reduced. I haven't completely done away with the little white pills, but the co-codomol is no longer on my monthly prescription request, and it has been several months since I have needed a maximum daily dose of anything. It is quite common not to have any discomfort for a day or two, but there are many things that I do which remind me that things have not fully recovered yet. Working up a step ladder invariably results in a period of pain, digging in the garden or chopping logs for the fire almost always makes my thigh hurt, and the scar still itches if I try to do things that involve lifting and carrying too much.

You need a new hip

The muscles in my leg are regaining their strength and the flesh around the scar is growing back, but I don't think I will ever swim or sunbathe in small trunks that expose that area of my body again.

The operation on my hip seems to have been a success, but on a slightly negative note I am having more and more discomfort from my left knee. I am still slow to sit down or stand up, and often groan if I kneel or stoop down, but now it's because of the knee rather than my hip. My knee was always going to cause me problems eventually after such a long time avoiding serious exercise, but so far the pain is nothing compared to the agony I had from my hip before it was replaced.

So that brings my story up to date, and hopefully anyone who is waiting for a hip replacement, or is in recovery from one, can get some comfort from my experiences over the last twelve months. Remember that everyone is different, and results vary from person to person. As I have tried to say already, expectations vary and some people will be more than happy just to have less pain than before the operation, or perhaps just to be able to walk again. Others may only be satisfied with no pain and full mobility again.

My recommendation would be to talk to your consultant and really discuss your hopes and expectations before signing the consent form. The majority of these procedures are successful and give the patient what they want, but the list of possible problems and side effects of the operation are stated very clearly before you can commit to a hip replacement.

So if you are one of the thousands of people who have a new hip each year, I wish you all the luck in the world.

You need a new hip

Oh No!

Things seemed to be going so well, but that pain in the groin just wouldn't go away. I eventually went to see my doctor at the end of August 2015 for some advice.

At least he assured me that the problem was almost certainly nothing to do with my hip replacement and everything suggested that it was my hernia.

I am about to start all over again with an appointment to see a consultant about an Inguinal Hernia. At least the waiting time is much shorter than anticipated and I will be seeing him at the beginning of October.

Of course the timing couldn't be worse as the balance of the fare for the world cruise has to be pain just a week later.

Surely I won't have to cancel it again!

Other books by the author

A Cornishman Goes Cruising

The reader will first be taken through the planning and preparation stages of a supposed one-off holiday of a lifetime, before travelling with the author and his wife on a magical adventure that changed their lives.

For those of you who have already sampled a cruise holiday, this will bring back the memories of life on board a ship, with all the choices available, and the thrill of waking up to a new location each day.

Perhaps you are considering a cruise.........Then this book will give you a flavour of the delights that can be expected on a fortnight's escape from normal everyday life.

Around the World without Wings

The author and his wife retired at the end of 2011 and they needed something really special to celebrate this moment.

So on a cold January evening in 2012 they left Southampton on the cruise ship MV Aurora on an adventure that would change their outlook on life, with a circumnavigation of the world lasting over three months.

Travel with them and share their thrills, laughter, and yes a few tears, as they discover so many amazing countries, cultures, and experiences on their journey around the world.

You need a new hip

A Cornishman Cruises to Venice

Venice has become one of the author's favourite cities in Europe, and hence is a regular port of call on the couple's summer cruises. As well as the beauty and magic when visiting this Italian gem, the book also explores the nearby historical city of Dubrovnik.

George and Deb always begin and end their cruises at Southampton, so the book spends time talking about the different ports that are also visited on the way to and from the Adriatic.

A Cornishman cruises the Western Mediterranean

The cruise ship adventures of the author and his wife (Deb) have visited many of the wonderful mainland Mediterranean ports of Spain, France and Italy, as well as numerous islands.

This volume of the Cornishman's maritime holidays, concentrates on the Western Mediterranean destinations.

Time for Tea and a Cheese Scone

Retirement at the end of 2011 brought new challenges for George and Deb, as well as the freedom from work.

The author kept a diary of the first year of retirement after over forty years of employment, and this book looks at the winter months as the couple get used to a new way of life.

You need a new hip

Would You like Some Plums?

Following on from the first book about their retirement, this book looks at the summer months in 2013.

As the couple enjoy their release from work, they decide to move to a new home.

Along with so many different things that the couple experienced in that six months, the house move becomes a major topic of this book.

A Cornish Boy Grows Up

This book is a rework of a previous book entitled See 'e 'gen Cornwall. Although much of the material is the same, the emphasis is on the author's early years, and school life until he begins full time employment.

George Williams was born in Cornwall at a time when life was far simpler and slower than children experience today. Holidaymakers come in their thousands to Cornwall each summer, to enjoy the golden beaches, but many also become fascinated by the County's Myths and Legends. Tiny fishing villages are full of locals speaking in an accent that is both sweet and confusing to a visitor's ear, and stories are recounted of Pirates and Piskies while they eat the famous pasties or cream teas.

The author grew up with his parents and three brothers, and life was full of fun with a small group of friends, but there were also some dark moments and tragedies. The lazy Cornish way of life did little to encourage George to take his education very seriously, and by the time he left in 1968 he had only acquired a handful of qualifications to attract the interest of prospective employers.

In this book the author candidly recounts the first phase of his life, as he makes his way from infant innocence, through painful hormone changes of adolescence, to the realisation that growing up means more than playtime. He also tries to give a flavour of Cornwall's uniqueness and beauty to those who have never sampled its delights, and attempts to share his love for the County.

Printed in Poland
by Amazon Fulfillment
Poland Sp. z o.o., Wrocław